HOW TO CHOOSE
and
HOW TO USE
a
DICTIONARY

Also by William F. Russell, Ed.D.

Classics to Read Aloud to Your Children

More Classics to Read Aloud to Your Children

Classic Myths to Read Aloud

Family Learning: How to Help Your Children Succeed in School by Learning at Home

A *Family Learning* Guidebook

HOW TO CHOOSE *and* HOW TO USE *a* DICTIONARY

by William F. Russell, Ed.D.

FIRST WORD Learning Systems, Inc.

St. Charles, Illinois

Published by
First Word Learning Systems, Inc.
Publishing Division
37W222 Route 64, PMB203
St. Charles, Illinois 60175-1000

Printed in the United States of America

Cover design by Ann Gjeldum
Interior design by Paul Christenson

Publisher's Catalog-in-Publication
Provided by Quality Books, Inc.

Russell, William F., 1945–
How to choose and how to use a dictionary /
William F. Russell.—1st ed.
p. cm.—(Family learning guidebook ; #1)
Includes index
ISBN: 0-9657752-8-3

1. English language— Dictionaries—History and criticism. 2. Encyclopedias and dictionaries—History and criticism. 3. English language—Lexicography. I. Title.

PE1611.R87 1999 413'.028
QBI99-791

LCCN: 99-71309
First Edition

ACKNOWLEDGMENTS

The author and publisher are greatly indebted to the following people and agencies for their help and their permission to include the sample dictionary pages and excerpts that appear in this volume:

"Argument" entry and sample page from *The World Book Dictionary* © 2000 World Book, Inc. By permission of the publisher. www.worldbook.com

By permission. From *Merriam-Webster's Collegiate® Dictionary, 10th Edition* © 1999 by Merriam-Webster, Incorporated.

Copyright © 1996 by Houghton Mifflin Company. Reproduced by permission from *The American Heritage Dictionary of the English Language, Third Edition.*

Copyright © 1997 by Houghton Mifflin Company. Reproduced by permission from *The American Heritage College Dictionary, Third Edition.*

Copyright © 1999 by Houghton Mifflin Company. Reproduced by permission from *Webster's II New College Dictionary.*

From *Oxford American Dictionary and Language Guide.* Copyright © 2000 by Oxford University Press, Inc. Used by permission of Oxford University Press, Inc.

Page reproduced from the US print edition of the *Encarta World English Dictionary.* The *Encarta World English Dictionary* is published in print form in the USA and Canada by St. Martin's Press, priced at $50, and in the UK, Europe and the rest of the world by Bloomsbury Publishing Plc, priced at £30 and in Australia, New Zealand and India by Macmillan. The Dictionary is published in electronic form worldwide by Microsoft Corporation. For more information: www.worldenglishdictionary.com

Random House, Inc. for *Random House Webster's College Dictionary*, Copyright ©1999, and *Webster's American Family Dictionary*, Copyright ©1999.

Reprinted with the permission of Macmillan General Reference, a wholly owned subsidiary of IDG Books Worldwide, Inc., from *Webster's New World College Dictionary, Fourth Edition* by Editor-in-Chief: Michael Agnes, Copyright © 1999, 1997, 1996, 1994, 1991, 1988 by Macmillan USA.

TABLE OF CONTENTS

HOW TO USE THIS BOOK

Each book in the *Family Learning* Guidebook series is patterned after the principles and practices found in *Family Learning: How to Help Your Children Succeed in School by Learning at Home*, by William F. Russell, Ed.D. Each guidebook focuses on a specific area of study that can be beneficial to parents and children alike, and each contains numerous "learning adventures" and family-centered, out-of-school learning activities that parents can share with their school-age children.

Two symbols appear frequently in the outside margins of this guidebook:

The "magnifying glass" symbol  appears wherever the text suggests specific words for readers to investigate in their "family dictionary." The words to be investigated also appear next to the symbol.

The "active family" symbol 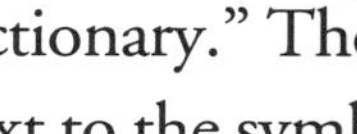 alerts parents to descriptions in the text of learning activities that they can share with their children. Each of these activities is summarized in the box containing the symbol.

CHOOSING A DICTIONARY

"Dictionaries are
like watches; the worst is
better than none,
and the best cannot be
expected to go quite true."

Samuel Johnson

If you were about to buy a computer, or a bicycle, or an outboard motor, a competent sales person would inquire about how you were intending to use the product before suggesting various models for you to consider. So, too, with a dictionary.

Do you just want to look up the accepted spellings of words you are writing in letters and reports? Do you just need a hard-copy backup resource for those occasions when your computer's spell-check program isn't working? Do you need an authoritative reference to use for language games and controversies that crop up from time to time ("But *gotcha* isn't a real word!")?

Well, there is good news for those of you who will be using a dictionary in these ways most of the time. First, there are inexpensive, paperbound, "pocket" dictionaries that will handle most of your spelling needs. There are also several "special" dictionaries that are specifically designed for use with Scrabble™ and other word games.

In fact, there are "special" dictionaries that are specifically designed for just about any use you can imagine—biographical dictionaries, geographical dictionaries, dictionaries to accompany the study of chemistry or mathematics, dictionaries of mythology, of music, of baseball—all called *dictionaries* because of their alphabetical arrangement and because they help you learn and understand the special vocabulary of words, phrases, people, and places that is used in each particular field.

For most of us, however, the particular field we want to better understand is the English language—its vocabulary, spellings, pronunciations, and word usage. We want a book that we can rely upon to unreproachfully alleviate our ignorance or clear up our confusion when we hear or read unfamiliar words. We want a book that will help us increase our command of English so that we won't feel reluctant to express ourselves or embarrassed by the form that our expression takes.

We also want to help our children acquire a command of language that will serve them well in any setting, whether social or business or educational.

We want a book that will provide an authoritative model for their language education—a counterweight to the standardless, "anything goes" message of the common culture that seems to be everywhere in their lives.

What we want, then, is a dictionary for the whole family—a "family dictionary"—that will meet our current language learning needs and will still be a valuable resource and guide as the frequency and difficulty of our demands increase from year to year.

Well, if this is how you intend to use a dictionary in your home, then there is good news as well, and the best news is that this *Family Learning Guidebook* has been designed with you in mind. The dictionaries that are described in the following pages are among the finest self-help, home-learning books ever produced, and although any one of them would be a useful and valuable addition to your home, they are different in many ways, and so you can tailor your choice to fit your particular preferences.

None of these dictionaries, however, will provide everything you need to guide your study of English and improve your children's use of language. Dictionaries are simply not designed to tell you *how* to improve your spelling, your pronunciation, your vocabulary, your word usage. Nor will a dictionary—any dictionary—give you much help in understanding *why* a word is spelled as it is, pronounced as it is, or frequently misused in speaking or writing. For these tasks you will need other resources (many of which I have suggested in the "Language" unit of *Family Learning*; others are listed in the "Useful Family Resources" section at the end of this book).

A dictionary provides the *what* in our quest for language improvement—the tens of thousands of words that can be used in hundreds of thousands of ways to help us convey clearly and artfully any idea we might ever want to express to anyone else in speech or writing. It is, perhaps, the one, indispensable language resource book for every home and family. But before we can profit from all the knowledge that is packed into this wonderful resource, before we can use a dictionary to answer our questions about language, we must first understand and become familiar with the way in which the particular dictionary we are reading chooses to tell us what we want to know.

> **A dictionary... is, perhaps, the one, indispensable language resource book for every home and family.**

Different Dictionaries Really Are Different

Most children—and most adults, too, I would guess—assume that there is something called "*the* dictionary," and that every dictionary that resides in a classroom or in a library or a in home is a more-or-less identical copy of that revered, prototypical work. It is because of this assumption that you will commonly hear or read phrases like "the dictionary says..." or "the dictionary defines..." followed by the particular piece of information that the speaker or writer wishes you to accept as indisputable fact. A variation on this theme is "Webster's defines the word..." and again the intention is to bestow absolute authority on a definition simply through the invocation of the name "Webster."

Well, let's spend just a moment examining the question of whether anything like "*the* dictionary" actually exists and what the name "Webster" has come to mean.

From the time that Noah Webster—a teacher and lawyer from Hartford, Connecticut—first published his *American Dictionary of the English Language* in 1828, and continuing up to about forty years ago, it could be fairly said that there really was one standard for dictionaries, and that standard was "Webster's." Indeed, by the end of World War II, the success of the 1934 version called *Webster's New International Dictionary of the English Language, Second Edition* (often called simply *Webster's Second* or *Webster II*) had driven most of its competitors to the sidelines and had become *the* accepted authority—even in courtrooms—for settling questions of spelling, pronunciation, and word usage.

The publishers of this dictionary, the G. & C. Merriam Company of Springfield, Massachusetts, had bought the rights to Noah Webster's works after his death in 1843, and they hired Webster's son-in-law to prepare their first "Merriam-Webster" dictionary in 1847. Every new edition, right up to *Webster's Second* in 1934, could trace its heritage, authority, and reputation to the great Noah Webster.

But during the 1940's, the World Publishing Company decided to challenge G. & C. Merriam's exclusive right to use the name "Webster." After several years of legal wrangling, the federal courts ruled in 1949 that the name "Webster" could not be any one company's property because it had entered the public domain (just like *aspirin*, *cellophane*, *kerosene*, and *escalator*, which also lost their status as protected trademarks). This decision cleared the way for the World Publishing Company to bring out its unabridged *Webster's New World Dictionary* in 1951 and *Webster's New World Dictionary, College Edition*, in 1953.

- ***aspirin***
- ***cellophane***
- ***kerosene***
- ***escalator***

Today, the G. & C. Merriam Company still claims that its "Webster's" dictionaries, unlike the "Webster's" dictionaries produced by other publishers, are directly descended from Noah Webster's original work, but all you need to understand about this legal and corporate dispute over the meaning and use of the name "Webster" is that its presence or absence in the title of a dictionary should not be a factor in choosing the right dictionary for you and your family. There simply are more important things to consider.

The considerations that should affect your choice of a dictionary pertain to the way that dictionary will be used at home.

Descriptive vs. Prescriptive

All of the considerations that really should affect your choice of a dictionary pertain, once again, to the way in which you intend to use that dictionary in your home. For example, if you are looking for a dictionary that will be a reliable authority for how words *should be* pronounced, as opposed to how they *are* pronounced most frequently, then you will want to choose a dictionary that provides you with this type of knowledge and guidance. What? You thought that's what *all* dictionaries did? Well, they used to—at least when *the* dictionary existed years ago, *it* used to.

Before the 1960's, almost all dictionary publishers followed Noah Webster's belief that a dictionary should serve, first of all, as a guidebook to aid in the self-education of the American people. Its primary function, therefore, was to guide, and so dictionary writers and editors, who are known as lexicographers [pronounced LEX-IH-CAH-GRUH-FURS], chose to include words, pronunciations, and spellings that *should be* used in educated speaking and writing. Look in the pages of *Webster's Second* (1934) or any of the subsequent "Webster's Collegiate" dictionaries that were based on it, and you'll find no mention at all of the word *ain't. Ain't* had been a common word in both speech and writing for hundreds of years, but the editors at G. & C. Merriam Company decided that it did not belong in a language "guide-book," and that was that. Similarly, the word *irregardless*, which is mistakenly used by people as a synonym for *regardless*, does not appear in these dictionaries because its very use is, in most cases, a mistake. You will not find profane words in these dictionaries, nor vulgar words, nor obscenities, and very little slang, as well. These words obviously existed, but they didn't exist in the dictionary because the purpose of the dictionary was to "prescribe" a standard for acceptable American English.

The 1960's brought about great change in many facets of American life, and so it is no surprise that this should be a watershed decade in the writing and publishing of dictionaries, as well. Indeed, 1961 marks the beginning of the greatest period of upheaval and change that the dictionary world had ever seen, and it all started with the publication of *Webster's Third New International Dictionary of the English Language* (commonly called *Webster's Third* or *Webster III*).

Webster's Third was a massive undertaking; it was the first dictionary written from scratch—that is, not based on any other work—in almost thirty years. It included over 450,000 entry words in its 2,662 pages, weighed over 14 pounds, and was the most controversial book of its day. It divided the literary world into two distinct and equally zealous camps: those who saw it as a great scholastic and intellectual achievement, and those who saw it as a subversive book that would lead to the ruination of the English language.

How could one book—and a dictionary, to boot—affect people so strongly and in such different ways?

Well, *Webster's Third* chose to shake the foundations on which *the* dictionary had rested for centuries. This new dictionary did not tell people how words *should be* spelled, pronounced, or used; instead, its purpose from the very beginning was to report about and describe how words actually *are* spelled, pronounced, and used by people in everyday speaking and writing. The lexicographers who compiled and edited *Webster's Third* believed that "prescriptive" dictionaries (those that prescribed language standards) were elitist and derogatory, while their "descriptive" dictionary would be more honest and democratic. If people didn't understand the distinction between *imply* and *infer*, or between

- ***imply***
- ***infer***
- ***flout***
- ***flaunt***

flout and *flaunt*, they reasoned, it was not the dictionary's duty to condemn their ignorance, and so *Webster's Third* listed each of these pairs as synonyms. Words that *Webster's Second* had labeled "colloquial" or "slang" bore no cautionary usage label at all in the pages of *Webster's Third.* Other labels, such as "illiterate" and "vulgar," were replaced by softer, less accusatory ones, such as "nonstandard" and "substandard." So, *irregardless* not only became one of the 450,000 entry words, it was labeled merely "nonstandard" and defined as another way of saying *regardless.* And *ain't* received an even greater elevation in stature, being described in *Webster's Third* as a word "used orally in most parts of the U.S. by many cultivated speakers."

- *irregardless*
- *regardless*
- *ain't*

A *New York Times* editorial in October, 1961, spoke for many who saw the permissiveness of this dictionary as being symbolic of the assault on standards of all kinds that was taking place in the country: "Webster's has, it is apparent, surrendered to the permissive school that has been busily extending its beachhead on English instruction in the schools. This development is disastrous because...it serves to reinforce the notion that good English is whatever is popular."

So, what kind of dictionary do you want in your home, a "prescriptive" one or a "descriptive" one?

Do you want your dictionary to tell you how language *should be* used or how language *is* used?

Almost every parent to whom I have posed these questions in workshops and speeches has voiced a decided preference for a "prescriptive" dictionary; that is, a guidebook that will help adults and children cultivate a better use of language. However, since the publication of *Webster's Third*, almost the entire dictionary world has gravitated to the position that the purpose of a dictionary is primarily to describe the way that language is actually used, not to prescribe how it should be used. And we can better understand why they have chosen this course when we delve a little further into what we want our "prescriptive" dictionary to do.

For example, if you want to know which spelling, pronunciation, or usage is "proper" or "preferred," ask yourself, "Preferred by whom?" Whose pronunciations should we try to adopt for ourselves, those of Boston-area professors? writers from the deep South? movie stars? professional athletes?

Fortunately for all of us, this "prescriptive" vs. "descriptive" debate among dictionary publishers and among dictionary buyers since *Webster's Third* hit the market has resulted in a general meeting of the minds that has proved quite beneficial to all concerned. Almost all "college size" or "desk size" dictionaries today have solved the dilemma by including the language as it is commonly used, but also providing guidance and knowledge about the various restrictions that limit the way language is used in various situations. Usage and status labels—such as *obsolete, chiefly British, informal, slang,* and *vulgar*—let the reader know that a certain pronunciation, spelling, or usage carries with it some additional baggage that may make it inappropriate for use in various settings. *Can* you still use words that carry qualifications like these? Of course you *can.* But usage labels offer you additional information to help you decide whether you will *want* to use the words in certain situations. These labels help you make a more informed decision, and that is exactly the kind of help you would expect to find in a guidebook.

Most dictionaries today also include special paragraphs that group several similar words together so that you can learn the precise meanings and the delicate distinctions that identify and separate each apparent synonym. Often there are "usage notes," as well, in which common and frequently troublesome problems in grammar and word choice are discussed. Again, the guidebook function of the dictionary—even though it is a "descriptive" dictionary—is addressed by providing you information on which you can make a choice about your own standards for usage.

Bigger Isn't Necessarily Better

How big should a "family dictionary" be? The answer to this question, as with so many other decisions in choosing a dictionary, depends upon how you intend to use it. Actually, the first question is *with whom* do you intend to use it, because the physical size and weight of some dictionaries make them difficult to handle and to pass around among family members.

The largest dictionaries in the general marketplace are called "unabridged" dictionaries—a term that simply means that the book is not a condensed version of a larger work. Unabridged dictionaries generally contain more than 300,000 main entries (boldface headwords that are pronounced and defined), but does this mean they include all the words in the English language? Not by a long shot.

No one knows how many words our language includes—millions, that's for sure. Why, every single species of insect has its own name, and there are more than 1.4 million of those names alone. Every chemical compound and protein chain can be described in words as well as symbols; one of those proteins—$C_{1289}H_{2051}N_{343}O_{375S8}$—spells a single word that is 1,913 letters long! Throw in the millions of names for various flora and fauna, medical conditions, technical and regional terms, and you have a total word stock that is both gigantic and meaningless.

The number of words in the vocabulary of the average, well-read, American adult has been estimated in various studies to be somewhere between 15,000 and 30,000 words. (But that person *uses* only 1,500 to 2,000 of those words in a week's worth of speaking, writing, and listening.) Even at best, that's only ten percent of the vocabulary contained in an unabridged dictionary. Yet, the main reason for not choosing an unabridged dictionary to be your "family dictionary" has more to do with the size of the book than the size of its vocabulary.

No one knows how many words our language includes—millions, that's for sure.

When you see an unabridged dictionary at the public library, you will almost always find it perched on a pedestal or on a swivel-based table stand of some kind. This is due to the fact that the book is both big and heavy—usually ten or twelve pounds. It is not a book that you can conveniently take to the place where you are doing your investigating; you must, instead, take your investigation to the book.

And that is precisely the problem with using such a massive book in your home: Its very size discourages its use. When you hear a strange word said during a television show, or when you question a particular usage that you have just read in the newspaper, you want to make your search for knowledge as convenient as possible, or else you will likely put the search off until later, and then forget about it altogether. You also want to be able to share your new knowledge with other family members, and you want them to be able to share the fruits of their investigations with you. But it's not easy to pass this big, heavy book from person to person (especially if some of those persons are children or grandparents), and so an unabridged dictionary usually stays where it was put in a home—upstairs, out of the way; a very expensive, but unused, learning resource.

There is, however, a style of dictionary that is ideally suited to use in the home, and dictionaries of this type are much less expensive than the unabridged ones, as well. Often called "semi-unabridged," these dictionaries typically contain 150,000 to 250,000 main entries and are often called "desk size" or "college" dictionaries. Most were designed with the college market in mind, and so they include a wide-ranging vocabulary that college students in a wide range of disciplines are likely to encounter in their studies. "They have three main benefits," says Kenneth G. Wilson, a lexicographer and University of Connecticut English professor. "They're inexpensive, they're portable, and above all, they're current."

There is so much competition between publishers in this market that prices are kept comparatively low and new editions come out frequently—almost every year or two. These rapid revisions and printings allow each dictionary to add the most current words and definitions almost as soon as they come into the language.

New Words

Is it important to you that the newest words and usages be included in your "family dictionary"? Well, I can picture a parent who is somewhat less than knowledgeable about the latest issues in computers and technology, and I can easily understand how that parent might want to have his or her dictionary be able to explain what a newscaster or a neighbor meant by "Y2K," "downloading," or "home page." All of us understand how much easier it is to alleviate our ignorance in the privacy of our own home than it is to ask someone for a definition and thereby demonstrate conclusively how little we know.

This principle applies to children, too, although their embarrassment over ignorance of any kind seems to be much more limited than it is in most adults. But if a student hears a parent or a teacher talking about "Generation X" or "mad cow disease," and simply cannot figure out from the context what these words mean, even a dictionary that was published only five or ten years ago will be of little help.

So, the modernness of a dictionary's entries, meanings, and usage labels can be a valuable consideration in choosing your "family dictionary," but a cautionary note is appropriate here. Beware of dictionaries that include the very latest fad words, jargon, and slang just to appear "up to date." Sometimes the paper dust jacket will trumpet the number of "brand new entries" or the "up-to-the-minute vocabulary" of a book, as though currency were the most important feature to consider, instead of just one feature to consider. It is occasionally true, as well, that dictionary publishers reveal a political bias in their choice of which new words to include and how those words should be defined. When you detect a concern like this (look, for example, at the entries for "hot button" words such as *right-wing*, *homeschool*, or *herstory*), you might wonder how much trust and faith you can have in using this book as your family's primary language resource.

Beware of dictionaries that include the very latest fad words, jargon, and slang just to appear "up to date."

- *right-wing*
- *homeschool*
- *herstory*

I have dealt with the subject of vulgar words and offensive words in a section titled "But It's in the Dictionary!" later in this book (see pages 86–88), but I think it is important to point out here that almost all the "college" dictionaries today (except the *Webster's American Family Dictionary*, published by Random House; *Webster's II New College Dictionary*, published by Houghton Mifflin; and *The World Book Dictionary*) have made the decision to include obscenities and "gutter expressions" of all kinds in their list of entries. This decision was a direct result of their choosing to be "descriptive" instead of "prescriptive," for it is hard to deny that obscene and offensive words and phrases *do* exist and *are* used in the language today. It is also true that some words and some expressions are objected to and considered offensive only by certain groups and then only in certain situations. Most lexicographers have chosen not to "police" the language, but simply to report every matter to the "judge," who is you.

Choosing Your Personal Preferences

While the size and weight of an unabridged dictionary make it an unlikely candidate for selection as your "family dictionary," there are several other considerations that might help you choose the right dictionary for your home.

Print Size and Page Layout.

If a dictionary is difficult to read, it is a lot less likely to be read, and so one of the first considerations you should have is for the readability of the page. The size of type that is used in printing the entry words and definitions is important in this regard, but readability is determined by many other factors, as well. The spacing between each line, for example, may be so cramped that even a comparatively large type size may be difficult to read. Then, too, there are certain typefaces that are more appealing to some readers than they are to others. Even the layout of the page itself comes into play, with some publishers opting for three columns per page, while others use just two.

If a dictionary is difficult to read, it is a lot less likely to be read.

The readability and appearance of the page is a matter that you must decide according to your own individual preferences. You may even choose to keep a small magnifying glass next to your dictionary at all times and thereby reduce or eliminate the readability question altogether.

Guide Words.

Another preference that you may have for one dictionary over another pertains to the method each uses for displaying guide words at the top of each page. These words tell you the very first and the very last entry words that appear on that page. If you make wise use of these guide words to help you land at the exact page and column where your target word resides (and I hope you will), you may very well have a decided preference for one of the three systems that are commonly used.

1. Two guide words per page, one above the left-hand column, one above the right-hand column (see sample page from *The American Heritage Dictionary of the English Language, Third Edition*).
2. Two guide words per page, both displayed together above the far left-hand or the far right-hand column on the page (see sample page from *Webster's New World College Dictionary, Fourth Edition*).
3. One guide word per page, showing the first entry word on a left-hand page or the last entry word on a right-hand page (see sample page from *The World Book Dictionary*).

Pronunciations.

Each dictionary uses a slightly different set of symbols to convey in writing how various pronunciations sound in speech. You will become accustomed to the system that your dictionary uses without much difficulty, and there really is no one system that is markedly better than another.

There is, however, one consideration that may prove rather important: Is the key to these symbols and sounds placed so that you can locate it without turning a page, or does it appear only at the front or back of the book? Once again, the more difficult something is to locate, the less likely it is to be used.

There are also three systems that are used for showing which syllables receive stress when a word is pronounced. The most common one places an accent mark (′) after each syllable that receives stress; a lighter mark appears after a syllable that receives a secondary stress.

> **co·opera·tion** or **co-operation** (kō äp′ər ā′shən) ***n.*** ⟦LL *coopera-tio*⟧ **1** the act of cooperating; joint effort or operation **2** the association of a number of people in an enterprise for mutual benefits or profits **3** *Ecol.* an interaction between organisms that is largely beneficial to all those participating Also **co·öp′·era′·tion** —**co·op′era′·tion·ist** ***n.*** or **co-op′era′tionist**

from *Webster's New World College Dictionary, Fourth Edition*

The *Merriam-Webster Collegiate® Dictionary* and *The Concise Oxford Dictionary,* on the other hand, use a vertical stress mark (') in their pronunciations and place it *before* the syllable that receives the stress. Primary stress is shown by a mark at the top of the syllable, secondary stress by a mark at the bottom.

> **aficionado** /əˌfɪsjəˈnɑːdəʊ, -ˌfɪʃjə-/ ● **n.** (pl. **-os**) a person who is very knowledgeable and enthusiastic about an activity or subject.
> – ORIGIN C19 (denoting a devotee of bullfighting): from Sp., 'amateur', past part. of *aficioner* 'become fond of' used as a noun, based on L. *affectio*(*n-*) (see **AFFECTION**).

from *The Concise Oxford Dictionary, Tenth Edition*

The third system is used in *The DK Illustrated Oxford University* and *The Oxford American Dictionary and Language Guide.* It prints the entry word broken into syllables, and all the letters in the pronunciation are run together; an accent mark is placed over the vowel that receives the most stress.

am•a•teur•ish /áməchŏŏ́r, –chərish, tər–, –tə́r–/ *adj.* characteristic of an amateur, esp. unskillful or inexperienced. □□ **am•a•teur•ish•ly** *adv.* **am•a•teur•ish•ness** *n.*
am•a•to•ry /ámətawree/ *adj.* of or relating to sexual love or desire. [L *amatorius* f. *amare* love]
am•au•ro•sis /ámərṓsis/ *n.* the partial or total loss of sight, from disease of the optic nerve, retina, spinal cord, or brain. □□ **am•au•rot•ic** /–rótik/ *adj.* [mod.L f. Gk f. *amauroō* darken f. *amauros* dim]
a•maze /əmáyz/ *v.tr.* (often foll. by *at*, or *that* + clause, or *to* + infin.) surprise greatly; overwhelm with wonder (*am amazed at your indifference*; *was amazed to find them alive*). □□ **a•maze•ment** *n.* **a•maz•ing** *adj.* **a•maz•ing•ly** *adv.* **a•maz•ing•ness** *n.* [ME f. OE *āmasod* past part. of *āmasian*, of uncert. orig.]

from *The Oxford American Dictionary and Language Guide*

If you are comfortable using one of these systems and not another, you may want to include that fact in your considerations, but most people find it rather easy to adapt to the system their dictionary happens to use.

Definitions.

When a word has more than one definition, lexicographers and publishers have to arrange those definitions in some meaningful order. This is an easy matter when each definition demonstrates a different part of speech. For example, the word *level* can be used as a noun ("a measuring instrument used in carpentry"), an adjective ("keeping a level head in an emergency"), or a verb ("to make horizontal or flat"). Each definition would be listed following the part-of-speech label to which its use applies.

But what if a word has several definitions that all can be used as the same part of speech? Which should be placed first? which last? and why? For example, as a noun, the word *mouse* can mean "a small rodent," "a black eye," or "a device for controlling computer operations." How should these definitions be arranged?

Some dictionaries have chosen to list the definitions that show the way the word is most frequently used first, and the least frequently used last.

> **la•bel** (lā′bəl), *n.*, *v.*, **-beled, -bel•ing** or (*esp. Brit.*) **-belled, -bel•ling.** —*n.* **1.** an inscribed slip of paper, cloth, or other material, for attachment to something to indicate its manufacturer, nature, ownership, destination, etc. **2.** a short word or phrase descriptive of a person, group, intellectual movement, etc. **3.** a word or phrase indicating that what follows belongs in a particular category or classification, as the word *Physics* before a dictionary definition. **4.** a brand or trademark, esp. of a manufacturer of phonograph records, tape cassettes, etc. **5.** the manufacturer using such a label. **6.** a molding over a door or window. **7.** a radioactive or heavy isotope incorporated into a molecule for use as a tracer. **8.** a narrow horizontal heraldic band with downward extensions. —*v.t.* **9.** to affix a label to; mark with a label. **10.** to designate or describe by or on a label: *The bottle was labeled poison.* **11.** to put in a certain class; classify. **12.** to incorporate a radioactive or heavy isotope into (a molecule) in order to make traceable. —**la′bel•er,** *n.*

from *Webster's American Family Dictionary*

Others prefer a historical arrangement showing how the meaning of each word has evolved over time. The earliest use is always listed first, and the most modern use last.

> [1]**dome** \'dōm\ *n* [F, It, & L; F *dôme* dome, cathedral, fr. It *duomo* cathedral, fr. ML *domus* church, fr. L, house; akin to Gk *domos* house, Skt *dam*] (1513) **1** *archaic* **:** a stately building **:** MANSION **2 :** a large hemispherical roof or ceiling **3 :** a natural formation or structure that resembles the dome or cupola of a building **4 :** a form of crystal composed of planes parallel to a lateral axis that meet above in a horizontal edge like a roof **5 :** an upward fold in rock whose sides dip uniformly in all directions **6 :** a roofed sports stadium — **dom•al** \'dō-məl\ *adj*
> [2]**dome** *vb* **domed; dom•ing** *vt* (1876) **1 :** to cover with a dome **2 :** to form into a dome ~ *vi* **:** to swell upward or outward like a dome

from *Mirriam-Webster's Collegiate® Dictionary, Tenth Edition*

Sometimes the definitions will also show the approximate year or period that each particular meaning came into common use. Under this historical arrangement, for example, the "small rodent" meaning of mouse would be shown first (it came into English around the year 900), the "black eye" meaning second (1854), and the "computer device" meaning last (1965).

Which system do you prefer? There are certainly arguments that can be made for each, and so it is, in the end, a matter of personal preference. The system adopted by each of the sample dictionaries shown in this book is listed under the heading "Order of Definitions."

Illustrative Examples.

Another way that dictionaries differ in the definitions they provide is in the method that each chooses to illustrate or clarify the meaning and the use of an entry word. The word *deign* [pronounced DANE], for example, when used as a transitive verb (see pages 78–79) can be defined as follows: "to condescend to give; to vouchsafe." Even if you bothered to read through the definitions of *condescend* and *vouchsafe*, you still might not understand how to use the original word, *deign*, in a sentence.

• deign
• condescend
• vouchsafe

Some dictionary publishers, therefore, include staff-written examples of how words are used in context. These illustrative examples may appear as sentence fragments ("to *deign* no answer"), as complete sentences ("She did not *deign* even a nod to show that she had heard"), and occasionally as direct quotations from famous speakers and writers ("'Nor would we *deign* him burial of his men'—Shakespeare").

in•di•cate (ĭn′dĭ-kāt′) *vt.* **-cat•ed, -cat•ing, -cates.** [Lat. *indicare, indicat-*, to show : *in-*, in + *dicare*, to proclaim.] **1.** To show or point out <*indicate* the quickest route> **2.** To serve as a sign, symptom, or token of : SIGNIFY <"The cracking and booming of the ice *indicate* a change of temperature" —Thoreau> **3.** To suggest or demonstrate the need, expedience, or advisability of <A sagging roof *indicates* immediate repairs.> **4.** To express briefly <*indicated* our hopes> **—in′di•ca•to′ry** (-kə-tôr′ē, -tōr′ē) *adj.*

from *The DK Illustrated Oxford Dictionary*

The presence and the frequency of these illustrative examples may be a significant aid in improving your family's understanding and use of words, and so you may wish to put some emphasis on this consideration in selecting your "family dictionary." Whether these examples are staff-written or quotations, however, is a matter of personal preference and is undoubtedly less important than the question of how clearly they illustrate the intended meaning.

Word Origins.

Most "college" dictionaries provide information about how each entry word (or at least most entry words) came into the English language. Every word has a history because the language we call "English" today is really an amalgamation of words from a hundred or more other languages, and by learning about how a word came to mean what it does in English, we can better understand and remember its meaning and its spelling.

The origin and historical development of a word is called its *etymology* [pronounced ET-UH-MOLL-UH-JEE], which is a very useful word for all dictionary users—children and adults alike—to know. The brief etymologies that are shown with the definitions of an entry word often make use of special symbols and abbreviations in order to save space. The < symbol is frequently used to mean "derived from" or simply "from," while abbreviations such as *OE* and *LL* might stand for the language periods called "Old English" and "Late Latin." All the symbols and abbreviations that are used in a dictionary's etymologies are identified and explained either at the very front or the very back of the book.

> **gov•ern** (guv′ərn), *v.t.* **1.** to rule by right of authority, as a sovereign does: *to govern a nation.* **2.** to exercise a directing or restraining influence over; guide: *the motives governing a decision.* **3.** to hold in check; control: *to govern one's temper.* **4.** to serve as or constitute a law for: *the principles governing a case.* **5.** (of a word or class of words) to require the use of a particular form of (another word or class). **6.** to regulate the speed of (an engine) with a governor. **—*v.i.*** **7.** to exercise the function of government. **8.** to have predominating influence. [1250–1300; ME < OF *gouverner* < L *gubernāre* to steer (a ship) < Gk *kybernân* to steer] —**gov′ern•a•ble,** *adj.*

from *Random House Webster's College Dictionary*

If the presence of these etymologies ranks high among the items you will consider in choosing a "family dictionary," then you also might have a preference for how they appear on the page. In some dictionaries, they appear at the beginning of the definitions, immediately after the entry word. In others, they appear at the end of the last definition.

If word histories are important to you (and I hope they are), you may also want to choose a dictionary that goes beyond the brief, etymological sketches within the definitions by including full-paragraph explanations of word histories that are particularly interesting.

pock·et·book (pŏk′ĭt-bo͝ok′) *n.* **1.** A pocket-sized folder or case used to hold money and papers; a billfold. **2.** A purse; a handbag. **3.** Financial resources; money supply: *prices to fit your pocketbook.* **4.** Often **pocket book.** A pocket-sized, usually paperbound book. In this sense, also called *pocket edition.*

WORD HISTORY: The link between the senses "billfold, purse," and "pocket-sized book" of the word *pocketbook* can be clarified with a little historical information. The compound is first recorded in 1617 in the sense of "a small book designed to be carried in a pocket." It is only recently that such books have looked like the paperbound books we are familiar with; these early paperbacks were bound like any book but were smaller in size. The next recorded use of *pocketbook* (1685) is again for a book designed to fit in the pocket but this time used for notes or memoranda. The same word was then applied to a case that was shaped like a book and in which money or papers could be kept. Finally, the word *pocketbook* was transferred to yet another container for keeping things, a purse or handbag, rarely fitting in the pocket and not necessarily shaped like a book.

from *The American Heritage Dictionary of the English Language, Third Edition*

Even if your "family dictionary" includes a number of these commentaries, you may want to explore this interesting area of language study even further by looking for books like *The Story Behind the Word*, by Morton S. Freeman, and *Word Origins and Their Romantic Stories*, by Wilfred Funk, in the 422 section at your public library.

Synonym Studies.

Another way that a good "family dictionary" can help you help your children develop a sense of precision in their use of language is by including paragraph-length explanations of the ways in which words whose meanings seem to be very similar are actually quite different. These paragraphs usually list the several synonyms at the beginning and then proceed to compare the shades of meaning associated with each word.

> **ar|gu|ment** (är′gyə mənt), *n.* **1** a discussion by persons who disagree; dispute: *He won the argument by producing figures to prove his point.* **2** giving reasons for or against something; debate: *Let us not waste time in argument.* **SYN**: discussion. **3** a reason or reasons given for or against something: *His arguments in favor of a new school are very persuasive.* **SYN**: rationale. **4** a short statement or summary of what is in a book, poem, or the like. **SYN**: abstract, theme. **5** *Mathematics.* an independent variable on whose value the value of a function depends. [< Latin *argūmentum* < *arguere* make clear]
> —*Syn.* **1 Argument, controversy, dispute** mean presentation of varying opinions by persons who disagree on some question. **Argument** suggests an intellectual encounter in which each side uses facts and reasons to try to convince the other: *His strong arguments persuaded me to accept his conclusions.* **Controversy** tends to suggest a more or less formal argument between groups, often carried on in writing or speeches: *The controversy over American schools still continues.* **Dispute** suggests contradicting rather than reasoning, and applies to an argument marked by feeling: *The dispute over the property was settled in court.*

from *The World Book Dictionary*

You can find other books in the 422–428 sections of your public library that will help you in making these small but important distinctions between words of similar meaning. Among my favorites are *When Is a Pig a Hog?* by Bernice Randall, and *The Appropriate Word,* by J. N. Hook.

Usage Notes.

All good dictionaries provide usage labels or status labels to show how various words, definitions, spellings, and pronunciations are categorized or restricted in common usage. Certain spellings, for instance, are labeled *Brit.* when those spellings are commonplace in England but not so in the United States, and usages are labeled *archaic* when they were commonplace in the past but now are rarely heard or seen. Similarly, usages that are frowned upon in polite speech or edited writing are designated *nonstandard, colloquial, informal,* and *slang,* while even stronger appellations, such as *offensive, vulgar,* and *obscene,* are used to warn readers about usages that violate common standards of decency.

Many dictionaries, though, go beyond these simple descriptions to advise readers about particularly troublesome areas of grammar and usage. They include paragraph-length "Usage Notes" following the definition of words that are frequently misused.

> **nei•ther** (nē′*th*ər, nī′-) *adj.* Not one or the other; not either: *Neither shoe feels comfortable.* —*pron.* Not either one; not the one or the other: *Neither of the twins is here.* —*conj.* **1.** Not either; not in either case. Used with the correlative conjunction *nor*: *I got neither the gift nor the card.* **2.** Also not: *If he won't go, neither will she.* —*adv.* Similarly not; also not: *Just as you would not, so neither would they.* [ME < OE *nāwther, nāhwæther* (influenced by *æghwæther, ægther*, either; see EITHER) : *nā*, not; see **ne*** + *hwæther*, which of two; see **kʷo-***.]
>
> ***Usage Note:*** According to the traditional rule, *neither* is used only to mean "not one or the other of two." To refer to "none of several," *none* is preferred: *None* (not *neither*) *of the three opposition candidates would make a better president than the incumbent.* • The traditional rule also holds that *neither* is grammatically singular: *Neither candidate is having an easy time with the press.* However, it is often used with a plural verb, especially when followed by *of* and a plural: *Neither of the candidates are really expressing their own views.* • As a conjunction *neither* is properly followed by *nor*, not *or*, in formal style: *Neither prayers nor curses did any good.* See Usage Notes at **either, every, he¹, none, nor¹, or¹.**

from *The American Heritage College Dictionary, Third Edition*

Here the lexicographers get an opportunity to do even more teaching than their "prescriptive" predecessors did, for these "Usage Notes" present the argument in full, instead of just removing the questionable usage altogether. Readers are left to make choices for themselves, but those choices will at least be informed choices, based on knowledge both of the situation and of the alternatives that are available.

Pictorial Illustrations.

Seeing a drawing or a photograph of a *mace* may help you visualize what this "medieval war club" actually looked like, and so a pictorial illustration, in this case, is an aid to your understanding. But does a photograph of a bridge or a drawing of a clock really help anyone arrive at a better understanding of these entry words?

You must decide whether the pictures and illustrations in a dictionary are useful aids to your learning or just cosmetic additions that may be attractive but of limited educational value.

Encyclopedic Information.

A dictionary can't—and shouldn't be asked to—take the place of an encyclopedia or an atlas. But there are many instances in which you might need only a basic piece of information about a famous person (How did she spell her name?), a historic event (When did it occur?), or a place on the globe (Where is it located?). In cases like these, it is helpful to be able to consult your "family dictionary" first, and then move on to a fuller understanding of the person, event, or place by consulting an encyclopedia or an atlas.

Albany River. A river rising in western Ontario, Canada, and flowing about 982 km (610 mi) east and northeast to James Bay. It was an important fur-trading route.

al·ba·tross (ăl′bə-trôs′, -trŏs′) *n., pl.* **albatross** or **-tross·es. 1.** Any of several large, web-footed birds constituting the family Diomedeidae, chiefly of the oceans of the Southern Hemisphere, and having a hooked beak and long, narrow wings. **2. a.** A constant, worrisome burden. **b.** An obstacle to success. [Probably alteration (influenced by Latin *albus,* white) of *alcatras,* pelican, from Portuguese or Spanish *alcatraz,* from Arabic *al-ġaṭṭās* : *al,* the + *ġaṭṭās,* white-tailed sea eagle. Sense 2, after the *albatross* in *The Rime of the Ancient Mariner* by Samuel Taylor Coleridge, which the mariner killed and had to wear around his neck as a penance.]

al·be·do (ăl-bē′dō) *n., pl.* **-dos.** The fraction of incident electromagnetic radiation reflected by a surface, especially of a celestial body. [Late Latin, whiteness, from Latin *albus,* white. See **albho-** in Appendix.]

Al·bee (ôl′bē, ŏl′-, ăl′-), **Edward Franklin.** Born 1928. American playwright. Best known for *Who's Afraid of Virginia Woolf?* (1962), he won a Pulitzer Prize in 1967 for *A Delicate Balance* and in 1975 for *Seascape.*

from *The American Heritage Dictionary of the English Language, Third Edition*

Most "college" dictionaries today include a good deal of encyclopedic information, but some place these biographical and geographical references in their regular alphabetical sequence along with other entry words, while others put all encyclopedic information in separate supplements and appendixes at the back of the book. Still others employ a mixture of both systems.

Other Considerations.

Modern dictionaries also compete against each other on matters that have little to do with words or language at all. Today there is a host of supplementary information to be found in almost every dictionary, including tables of weights and measures, maps, population statistics, signs and symbols, style manuals for writing, and historic documents such as the *Declaration of Independence* and the *Constitution of the United States.*

All of these features can be found in other commonly available resources, and so you don't want to let them distract your focus from selecting a dictionary that will meet your needs and preferences *for a dictionary*, first and foremost. After that challenge is met, anything else that comes with the package is purely a bonus.

Ranking Your Preferences

So, which of these differences make a difference to you? You probably feel strongly about some, and don't care very much about others. Let's focus on those two or three or four that really do matter to you, and then let's see how the twelve dictionaries that I have described in this book measure up just on those considerations alone.

Turn to pages 70 and 71. Here you'll find a chart listing the titles of the twelve dictionaries that I consider "family dictionaries" across the top, and a series of questions down the left-hand side. Each question deals with a category or characteristic that I have explained in the previous pages and that I have used in compiling the features of each dictionary in the sample pages that follow. Which of these questions and categories is especially important to you?

Simply consult the list of features across from each dictionary's sample page, and then place a plus (+) or a minus (-) sign underneath each dictionary title in the chart, depending upon whether that particular dictionary meets your particular need in this particular area or preference.

Place marks only in the rows of categories about which you have a decidedly strong feeling or preference (mark these categories with an X in the "Important Preferences" column), or else you might find yourself marking a dictionary down for not having features that you didn't care whether it had in the first place.

SAMPLE PAGES FROM POPULAR "FAMILY DICTIONARIES"

The following section contains full-size reproductions of sample pages from the most popular "family dictionaries" on the market today. By comparing the layout, the type size, and the typeface found on these sample pages, you will be able to judge which ones are the most readable and appealing to you. (Note: The sample page from *The DK Illustrated Oxford Dictionary* appears in black and white only, although the illustrations in this dictionary are all in color.)

On the left side of each sample dictionary page there is a box with information pertaining to that particular dictionary. Here you will find a collection of facts describing how each dictionary treats pronunciations, definitions, synonyms, and all the other categories of preferences that are described in "Choosing a Dictionary"and are listed in the "Dictionary Preference Chart" on pages 70 and 71.

Title: **The American Heritage College Dictionary, Third Edition**
Publisher: **Houghton Miffin Company**
Most recent copyright: **1997**
Number of Volumes: **1**
Weight: **3lbs., 9 ozs.**
Price: **$24.00**

Type size (entry words / definitions): **6.9 pt / 6.9 pt**
Columns per page: **2**
Guide words per page: **2–both shown together**
Pronunciation keys: **every other page**
Method for accent marks: **after syllable**
Order of definitions: **frequency of use**
Illustrative examples: **yes**
Illustrative quotations: **yes**
Placement of etymologies: **after definitions**
Synonym studies: **yes**
Word history studies: **yes**
Usage studies: **yes**
Pictorial illustrations (number): **2,500**
Encyclopedic information: **in main body**

Special Features:

- **Usage Panel of writers and scholars offers guidance on language questions**
- **Notes concerning regional vocabularies and dialects**
- **Currency table**
- **Periodic table of elements**

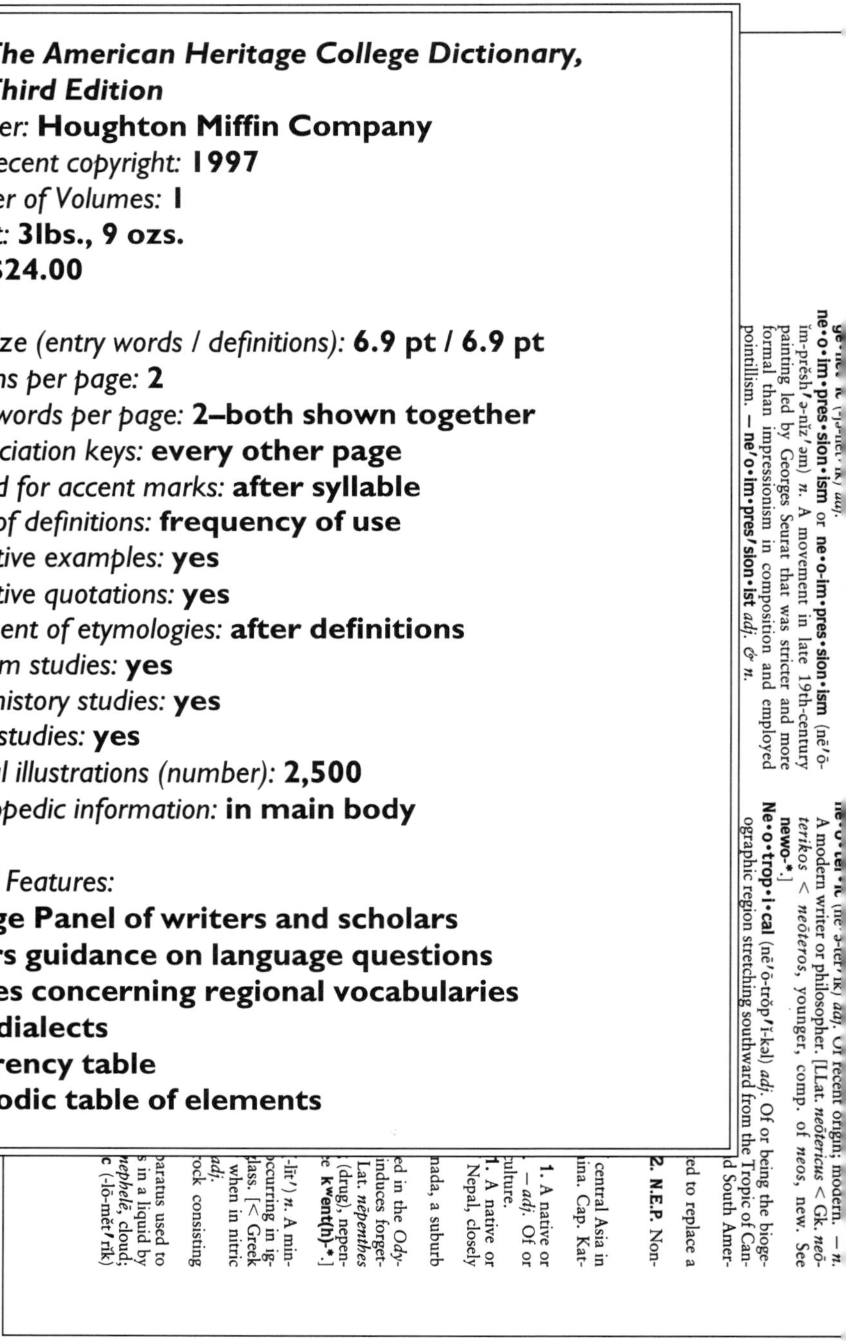

ne•o•im•pres•sion•ism or **ne•o-im•pres•sion•ism** (nē′ō-im-prĕsh′ə-nĭz′əm) *n.* A movement in late 19th-century painting led by Georges Seurat that was stricter and more formal than impressionism in composition and employed pointillism. — **ne′o•im•pres′sion•ist** *adj. & n.*

A modern writer or philosopher. [LLat. *neōtericus* < Gk. *neōterikos* < *neōteros*, younger, comp. of *neos*, new. See **newo-***.]

Ne•o•trop•i•cal (nē′ō-trŏp′ĭ-kəl) *adj.* Of or being the biogeographic region stretching southward from the Tropic of Cancer

neoclassicism
West Building of the National Gallery of Art in Washington DC, designed by John Russell Pope (1874 – 1937)

ne•o•clas•si•cism also **Ne•o•clas•si•cism** (nē′ō-klăs′ĭ-sĭz′-əm) *n.* A revival of classical aesthetics and forms, esp.: **a.** A revival in literature in the late 17th and 18th centuries characterized by a regard for the classical ideas of reason, form and restraint. **b.** A revival in the 18th and 19th centuries in architecture and art, esp. in the decorative arts, characterized by order, symmetry, and simplicity of style. **c.** A movement in music in the late 19th and early 20th centuries that sought to avoid subjective emotionalism and to return to the style of the pre-Romantic composers. **—ne′o•clas′sic, ne′-o•clas′si•cal** *adj.*

ne•o•co•lo•ni•al•ism (nē′ō-kə-lō′nē-ə-lĭz′əm) *n.* A policy whereby a major power uses economic and political means to perpetuate or extend its influence over underdeveloped nations or areas. **—ne′o•co•lo′ni•al** *adj.* **—ne′o•co•lo′ni•al•ist** *n.*

ne•o•con•ser•va•tism also **ne•o-con•ser•va•tism** (nē′ō-kən-sûr′və-tĭz′əm) *n.* An intellectual and political movement in favor of political, economic, and social conservatism that arose in opposition to the perceived liberalism of the 1960's. **—ne′o•con•ser′va•tive** *adj. & n.*

ne•o•cor•tex (nē′ō-kôr′tĕks′) *n., pl.* **-ti•ces** (-tĭ-sēz′) or **-tex•es.** The dorsal region of the cerebral cortex, esp. large in higher mammals and the most recently evolved part of the brain. **—ne′o•cor′ti•cal** (-tĭ-kəl) *adj.*

Ne•o-Dar•win•ism (nē′ō-där′wə-nĭz′əm) *n.* Darwinism as modified by the findings of modern genetics. **—Ne′o-Dar•win′i•an** (-där-wĭn′ē-ən) *adj.* **—Ne′o-Dar′win•ist** *n.*

ne•o•dym•i•um (nē′ō-dĭm′ē-əm) *n. Symbol* **Nd** A rare-earth element found in monazite and bastnaesite and used for coloring glass and doping some glass lasers. Atomic number 60; atomic weight 144.24; melting point 1,024°C; boiling point 3,027°C; specific gravity 6.80 or 7.004 (depending on allotropic form); valence 3. See table at **element.** [NEO– + (DI)-DYMIUM.]

ne•o•fas•cism (nē′ō-făsh′ĭz′əm) *n.* A fringe movement inspired by the tenets and methods of fascism or Nazism. **—ne′o•fas′cist** *adj. & n.*

Ne•o-Freud•i•an (nē′ō-froi′dē-ən) *adj.* Of, relating to, or characterizing any psychoanalytic system based on but modifying Freudian doctrine by emphasizing social factors, interpersonal relations, or other cultural influences in personality development or causation of the neuroses. **—Ne′o-Freud′i•an** *n.*

Ne•o•gae•a also **Ne•o•ge•a** (nē′ə-jē′ə) *n.* A region that is coextensive with the Neotropical region and is considered one of the primary biogeographic realms. [NLat. : NEO– + Gk.

ne•o•na•tol•o•gy (nē′ō-nā-tŏl′ə-jē) *n.* The branch of pediatrics that deals with the diseases and care of newborn infants. **—ne′o•na•tol′o•gist** *n.*

ne•o-Na•zi (nē′ō-nät′sē, -năt′-) *n.* A member of a fringe group inspired by Adolf Hitler's Nazis. **—ne′o-Na′zism** *n.*

neon tetra *n.* A small tropical freshwater fish *(Hyphessobrycon innesi)* of the Amazon River having blue and red markings.

ne•o-or•tho•dox•y (nē′ō-ôr′thə-dŏk′sē) *n.* A Protestant movement arising during World War I that opposes liberalism and favors Calvinism. **—ne′o-or′tho•dox′** *adj.*

ne•o•phyte (nē′ə-fīt′) *n.* **1.** A recent convert to a belief; a proselyte. **2.** A beginner or novice. **3.a.** *Rom. Cath. Ch.* A newly ordained priest. **b.** A novice of a religious order or congregation. [ME < LLat. *neophytus* < Gk. *neophutos* : *neo-*, neo- + *-phutos*, planted (< *phuein*, to bring forth; see **bheuə-***).]

ne•o•pla•sia (nē′ō-plā′zhə, -zhē-ə) *n.* **1.** Formation of new tissue. **2.** Formation of a neoplasm or neoplasms.

ne•o•plasm (nē′ə-plăz′əm) *n.* An abnormal new growth of tissue; a tumor. **—ne′o•plas′tic** (-plăs′tĭk) *adj.*

Ne•o-Pla•to•nism also **Ne•o•pla•to•nism** (nē′ō-plāt′n-ĭz′-əm) *n.* **1.** A philosophical system developed in the third century A.D. that is based on Platonism with elements of mysticism and some Judaic and Christian concepts and posits a single source from which all existence emanates and with which an individual soul can be mystically united. **2.** A revival of Neo-Platonism or a system derived from it, as in the Middle Ages. **—Ne′o-Pla•ton′ic** (-plə-tŏn′ĭk) *adj.* **—Ne′o-Pla′-to•nist** *n.*

ne•o•prene (nē′ə-prēn′) *n.* A synthetic rubber produced by polymerization of chloroprene and used in weather-resistant products, adhesives, shoe soles, paints, and rocket fuels. [NEO– + (CHLORO)PRENE.]

Ne•o-Scho•las•ti•cism (nē′ō-skə-lăs′tĭ-sĭz′əm) *n.* A chiefly Roman Catholic intellectual movement that arose in the late 19th century and seeks to revive medieval Scholasticism by infusing it with modern concepts. **—Ne′o-Scho•las′tic** (-lăs′tĭk) *adj.*

Ne•o•sho (nē-ō′shō, -shə). A river rising in E-central KS and flowing c. 740 km (460 mi) to the Arkansas R. in E OK.

ne•o•stig•mine (nē′ō-stĭg′mēn, -mĭn) *n.* Either of two related white, crystalline cholinergic compounds, $C_{12}H_{19}BrN_2O_2$ or $C_{13}H_{22}N_2O_6S$, used in the treatment of glaucoma and myasthenia gravis. [NEO– + (PHYSO)STIGMINE.]

ne•ot•e•ny (nē-ŏt′n-ē) *n.* **1.** Retention of juvenile characteristics in the adults of a species. **2.** The attainment of sexual maturity by an organism still in its larval stage. [NLat. *neote-*

Title: ***The American Heritage Dictionary of the English Language, Third Edition***
Publisher: **Houghton Mifflin Company**
Most recent copyright: **1996**
No. of volumes: **1**
Weight: **6 lbs., 15 ozs.**
Price: **$50.00**

Type size (entry words / definitions): **7 pt / 6.5 pt**
Columns per page: **2**
Guide words per page: **2–shown on left and right**
Pronunciation keys: **every other page**
Method for accent marks: **after syllable**
Order of definitions: **frequency of use**
Illustrative examples: **yes**
Illustrative quotations: **yes**
Placement of etymologies: **after definitions**
Synonym studies: **yes**
Word history studies: **yes**
Usage studies: **yes**
Pictorial illustrations (number): **4,000**
Encyclopedic information: **in main body**

Special features:

- **Usage Panel of writers and scholars offers guidance on language questions**
- **Notes concerning regional vocabularies and dialects**
- **Currencies table**
- **Periodic table of elements**
- **Proofreaders' marks**

crenate

cre•nate (krē′nāt′) also **cre•nat•ed** (-nā′tĭd) *adj.* Having a margin with low, rounded or scalloped projections: *a crenate leaf.* [New Latin *crēnātus,* from Medieval Latin *crēna,* notch.] **—cre′nate′ly** *adv.*

cre•na•tion (krĭ-nā′shən) *n.* **1.** A rounded projection, as on the margin of a shell. **2.** The condition or state of being crenate. **3.** A process resulting from osmosis in which red blood cells, in a hypertonic solution, undergo shrinkage and acquire a notched or scalloped surface.

cren•a•ture (krĕn′ə-chər, krē′nə-) *n.* A rounded projection; a crenation.

cren•e•lat•ed also **cren•el•lat•ed** (krĕn′ə-lā′tĭd) *adj.* **1.** Having battlements. **2.** Indented; notched: *a crenelated wall.* [Probably from French *créneler,* to furnish with battlements, from Old French *crenel,* crenelation, diminutive of *cren,* notch. See CRANNY.] **—cren′e•la′tion** *n.*

cren•shaw (krĕn′shô′) *n.* A variety of winter melon *(Cucumis melo* var. *inodorus)* having a greenish-yellow rind and sweet, usually salmon-pink flesh. [Origin unknown.]

cren•u•late (krĕn′yə-lĭt, -lāt′) also **cren•u•lat•ed** (-lā′tĭd) *adj.* Having a margin with very small, low, rounded teeth: *a crenulate leaf.* [New Latin *crēnulātus,* from *crēnula,* diminutive of Medieval Latin *crēna,* notch.] **—cren′u•la′tion** *n.*

cre•o•dont (krē′ə-dŏnt′) *n.* Any of various extinct carnivorous mammals of the suborder Creodonta, of the Paleocene Epoch to the Pliocene Epoch. [From New Latin *Creodonta,* suborder name : Greek *kreas,* flesh; see **kreuə-** in Appendix + Greek *odous, odont-,* tooth.]

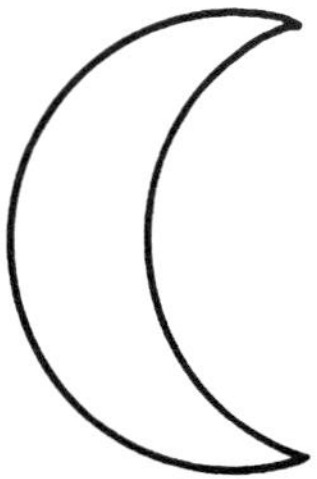

Cre•ole (krē′ōl′) *n.* **1.** A person of European descent born in the West Indies or Spanish America. **2.a.** A person descended from or culturally related to the original French settlers of the southern United States, especially Louisiana. **b.** The French dialect spoken by these people. **3.** A person descended from or culturally related to the Spanish and Portuguese settlers of the Gulf States. **4.** Often **creole.** A person of mixed Black and European ancestry who speaks a creolized language, especially one based on French or Spanish. **5.** A Black slave born in the Americas as opposed to one brought from Africa. **6. creole.** A creolized language. **7.** Haitian Creole. **—Creole** *adj.* **1.** Of, relating to, or characteristic of the Creoles. **2. creole.** Cooked with a spicy sauce containing tomatoes, onions, and peppers: *shrimp creole; creole cuisine.* [French *créole,* from Spanish *criollo,* person native to a locality, from Portuguese *crioulo,* diminutive of *cria,* person raised in the house, especially a servant, from *criar,* to bring up,

crepitāt-, to crackle, frequentative of *crepāre,* to creak.] **—crep′i•tant** (-tənt) *adj.* **—crep′i•ta′tion** *n.*

crept (krĕpt) *v.* Past tense and past participle of **creep.**

cre•pus•cle (krĭ-pŭs′əl) *n.* Variant of **crepuscule.**

cre•pus•cu•lar (krĭ-pŭs′kyə-lər) *adj.* **1.** Of or like twilight; dim: *"the period's crepuscular charm and a waning of the intense francophilia that used to shape the art market"* (Wall Street Journal). **2.** *Zoology.* Becoming active at twilight or before sunrise, as do bats and certain insects and birds.

cre•pus•cule (krĭ-pŭs′kyōōl) also **cre•pus•cle** (-pŭs′əl) *n.* Twilight. [Middle English, from Old French, from Latin *crepusculum,* from *creper,* dark.]

cres•cen•do (krə-shĕn′dō) *n., pl.* **-dos** or **-di** (-dē). **1.** *Abbr.* **cr.** *Music.* **a.** A gradual increase, especially in the volume or intensity of sound in a passage. **b.** A passage played with a gradual increase in volume or intensity. **2.a.** A steady increase in intensity or force: *"insisted* [that] all *paragraphs . . . should be structured as a crescendo rising to a climactic last sentence"* (Henry A. Kissinger). **b.** *Usage Problem.* The climactic point or moment after such a progression: *"The attacks . . . began in December . . . and reached a crescendo during* [the president's] *September visit"* (Foreign Affairs). **—crescendo** *adj.* Gradually increasing in volume, force, or intensity. **—crescendo** *adv.* *Music.* With a crescendo. **—crescendo** *intr.v.* **-doed, -do•ing, -does.** To build up to or reach a point of great intensity, force, or volume: *"The designer-name craze crescendoed in the mid-seventies"* (Bernice Kanner). [Italian, present participle of *crescere,* to increase, from Latin *crēscere.* See **ker-**[2] in Appendix.]

USAGE NOTE: *Crescendo* is sometimes used by reputable speakers and writers to denote a climax or peak, as in noise level, rather than an increase. Although citational evidence over time attests to widespread currency, it is difficult for anyone acquainted with the technical musical sense of *crescendo* to use it to mean "a peak." Such usage, as in *When the guard sank a three-pointer to tie the game, the noise of the crowd reached a crescendo,* was unacceptable to 55 percent of the Usage Panel.

cres•cent (krĕs′ənt) *n.* **1.** The figure of the moon as it appears in its first or last quarter, with concave and convex edges terminating in points. **2.** Something having concave and convex edges terminating in points. **—crescent** *adj.* **1.** Crescent-shaped. **2.** Waxing, as the moon; increasing. [Middle English *cressaunt,* from Anglo-Norman, variant of Old French *creissant,* from pre-

Title: **The Concise Oxford Dictionary, Tenth Edition**
Publisher: **Oxford University Press**
Most recent copyright: **1999**
No. of volumes: **1**
Weight: **3 lbs., 8 ozs.**
Price: **$29.95**

Type size (entry words / definitions): **7 pt / 6.5 pt**
Columns per page: **2**
Guide words per page: **2–both shown together**
Pronunciation keys: **every other page**
Method for accent marks: **before syllable**
Order of definitions: **frequency of use**
Illustrative examples: **yes**
Illustrative quotations: **no**
Placement of etymologies: **after definitions**
Synonym studies: **no**
Word history studies: **no**
Usage studies: **yes**
Pictorial illustrations (number): **none**
Encyclopedic information: **in main body**

Special features:

- **Primarily British vocabulary with U.S., Australian, Canadian usages labeled**
- **"Word Formation" charts show how groups of words have grown from same root**

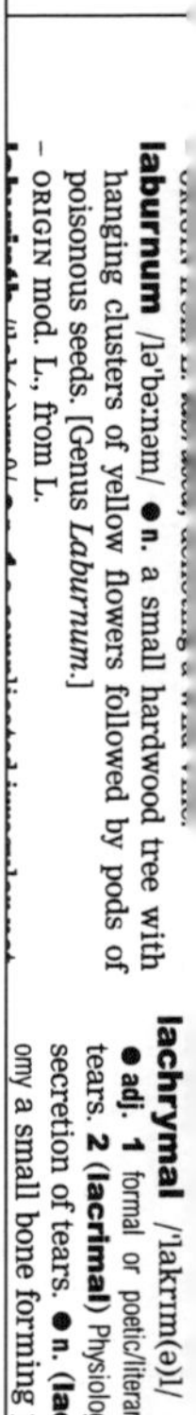

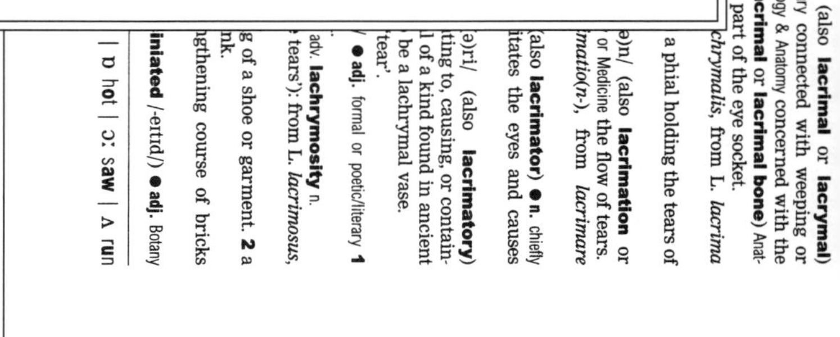

Labour Day | laciniate 792

Labour Day ● n. a public holiday held in honour of working people in some countries on 1 May, or (in the US and Canada) on the first Monday in September.

laboured (US **labored**) ● adj. **1** done with great difficulty. **2** not spontaneous or fluent.

labourer (US **laborer**) ● n. a person doing unskilled manual work.

labour exchange ● n. former term for **JOBCENTRE**.

labour force ● n. the members of a population who are able to work.

labour-intensive ● adj. needing a large workforce or a large amount of work in relation to output.

labourism (US **laborism**) ● n. the principles of a Labour Party or the labour movement.
– DERIVATIVES **labourist** n. & adj.

Labourite (US **Laborite**) ● n. a member or supporter of a Labour Party.

labour-saving ● adj. (of an appliance) designed to reduce or eliminate work.

labour theory of value ● n. the Marxist theory that the value of a commodity should be determined by the amount of human labour used in its production.

labour union ● n. chiefly N. Amer. a trade union.

labra plural form of **LABRUM**.

Labrador /ˈlabrədɔː/ (also **Labrador retriever**) ● n. a retriever of a breed typically having a black or yellow coat, widely used as a gun dog or guide dog.
– ORIGIN C20: named after the *Labrador* Peninsula of eastern Canada, where the breed was developed.

labradorite /ˌlabrəˈdɔːrʌɪt/ ● n. a mineral of the plagioclase feldspar group, found in many igneous rocks.

Labrador tea ● n. a low-growing northern shrub with fragrant leathery evergreen leaves, sometimes used in Canada to make tea. [Genus *Ledum*.]

labret /ˈleɪbrɪt/ ● n. a small piece of shell, bone, etc. inserted into the lip as an ornament in some cultures.
– ORIGIN C19: dimin. of **LABRUM**.

labrum /ˈleɪbrəm/ ● n. (pl. **labra** /-brə/) Zoology a structure corresponding to a lip, especially the upper border of the mouthparts of a crustacean or insect.
– DERIVATIVES **labral** adj.
– ORIGIN C18: from L., lit. 'lip'; rel. to **LABIUM**.

lac[2] ● n. variant spelling of **LAKH**.

Lacanian /laˈkeɪnɪən/ ● adj. of or relating to the French psychoanalyst and writer Jacques Lacan (1901–81). ● n. a follower of Lacan.
– DERIVATIVES **Lacanianism** n.

laccolith /ˈlakəlɪθ/ ● n. Geology a lens-shaped mass of igneous rock intruded between rock strata, causing doming.
– ORIGIN C19: from Gk *lakkos* 'reservoir' + **-LITH**.

lace ● n. **1** a fine open fabric of cotton or silk made by looping, twisting, or knitting thread in patterns, used especially as a trimming. ➤braid used for trimming, especially on military dress uniforms. **2** a cord or leather strip passed through eyelets or hooks to fasten a shoe or garment. ● v. **1** fasten or be fastened with a lace or laces. ➤tighten a laced corset around the waist of. ➤[as adj. **laced**] trimmed or fitted with a lace or laces. **2** entwine. **3** (often **be laced with**) add an ingredient, especially alcohol, to (a drink or dish) to enhance its flavour or strength. **4** (**lace into**) informal assail or tackle.
– ORIGIN ME: from OFr. *laz*, *las* (n.), *lacier* (v.), based on L. *laqueus* 'noose'; cf. **LASSO**.

lace bug ● n. a small plant-eating bug with a patterned upper surface. [Family Tingidae.]

Lacedaemonian /ˌlasɪdɪˈməʊnɪən/ ● n. a native or inhabitant of Lacedaemon, an area of ancient Greece comprising the city of Sparta and its surroundings. ● adj. of Lacedaemon or its inhabitants; Spartan.

lace pillow ● n. a cushion placed on the lap to provide support in lacemaking.

lacerate /ˈlasəreɪt/ ● v. tear or deeply cut (the flesh or skin).
– DERIVATIVES **laceration** n.
– ORIGIN ME: from L. *lacerat-*, *lacerare* 'mangle', from *lacer* 'torn'.

Lacertilia /ˌlasəˈtɪlɪə/ ● pl. n. Zoology a suborder of reptiles that comprises the lizards.
– DERIVATIVES **lacertilian** n. & adj.
– ORIGIN mod. L., from L. *lacerta* 'lizard'.

lacewing ● n. a slender delicate insect with large clear membranous wings, predatory on aphids. [Chrysopidae (**green lacewings**) and other families.]

lacewood ● n. the wood of the plane tree.

laches /ˈlatʃɪz, ˈleɪ-/ ● n. Law unreasonable delay in mak-

Title: **The DK Illustrated Oxford Dictionary**
Publisher: **DK Publishing**
Most recent copyright: **1998**
No. of volumes: **1**
Weight: **6 lbs., 7 ozs.**
Price: **$50.00**

Type size (entry words / definitions): **7 pt / 6.5 pt**
Columns per page: **3**
Guide words per page: **2–shown on left and right**
Pronunciation keys: **front only**
Method for accent marks: **above vowel**
Order of definitions: **frequency of use**
Illustrative examples: **yes**
Illustrative quotations: **no**
Placement of etymologies: **none**
Synonym studies: **no**
Word history studies: **no**
Usage studies: **yes**
Pictorial illustrations (number): **4,500 (full-color)**
Encyclopedic information: **in separate sections**

Special features:
- **250 in-depth visual definitions**
- **Grammar and style guide**
- **Four-color maps of the world and night sky**
- **Flags and countries of the world**
- **Geological time, time zones**
- **Tables of weights and measures, signs and symbols, chemical elements**

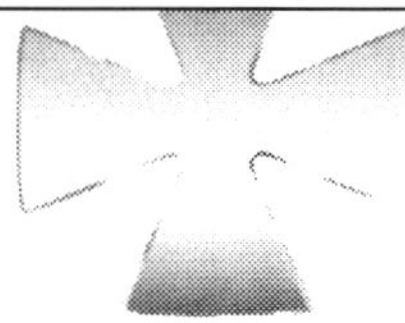

MAKO
(*Isurus oxyrinchus*)

ma·ko /máykō, maákō/ *n.* (*pl.* **-os**) ▲ a blue shark, *Isurus oxyrinchus.* ▷ SHARK

mal- /mal/ *comb. form* **1** bad; badly (*malpractice; maltreat*). **2** faulty; faultily (*malfunction*).

mal·ab·sorp·tion /máləbsáwrpshən, -záwrp-/ *n.* imperfect absorption of food by the small intestine.

ma·lac·ca /məlákə/ *n.* (in full **malacca cane**) a rich-brown cane from the stem of the palm tree *Calamus scipionum*, used for walking sticks, etc.

mal·a·chite /máləkīt/ *n.* ▶ a bright-green mineral of hydrous copper carbonate, used for ornament. ▷ GEM

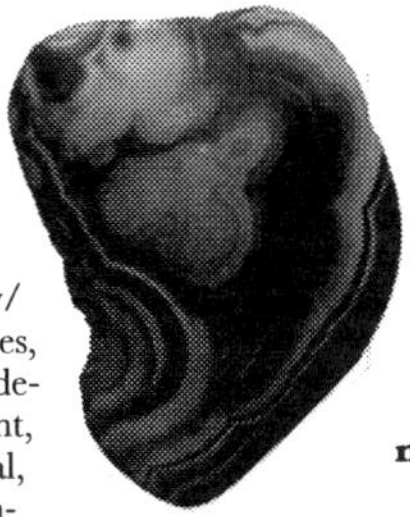

MALACHITE: BANDED VARIETY

mal·a·col·o·gy /máləkóləjee/ *n.* the study of mollusks.

mal·a·dap·tive /máladáptiv/ *adj.* (of an individual, species, etc.) failing to adjust adequately to the environment, and undergoing emotional, behavioral, physical, or mental repercussions. □□ **mal·a·dap·ta·tion** /máladaptáyshən/ *n.*

mal·ad·just·ed /máləjústid/ *adj.* **1** not correctly adjusted. **2** (of a person) unable to adapt to or cope with the demands of a social environment. □□ **mal·ad·just·ment** *n.*

mal·ad·min·is·ter /máladmínistər/ *v.tr.* manage badly. □□ **mal·ad·min·is·tra·tion** /-stráyshən/ *n.*

Ma·lay /máylay, məláy/ *n. & adj.* ● *n.* **1 a** a member of a people predominating in Malaysia and Indonesia. **b** a person of Malay descent. **2** the language of this people, the official language of Malaysia. ● *adj.* of or relating to this people or language. □□ **Ma·lay·an** *n. & adj.*

mal·con·tent /málkəntent/ *n. & adj.* ● *n.* a discontented person; a rebel. ● *adj.* discontented or rebellious.

male /mayl/ *adj. & n.* ● *adj.* **1** of the sex that can beget offspring by fertilization or insemination. (*male child; male dog*) **2** of men or male animals, plants, etc.; masculine. (*the male sex; a male-voice choir*) **3 a** (of plants or their parts) containing only fertilizing organs. **b** (of plants) thought of as male because of color, shape, etc. **4** (of parts of machinery, etc.) designed to enter or fill the corresponding female part (*a male plug*). ● *n.* a male person or animal. □□ **male·ness** *n.*

male chau·vin·ist (pig) *n.* a man who is prejudiced against women or regards women as inferior.

mal·e·dic·tion /málidíkshən/ *n.* **1** a curse. **2** the utterance of a curse.

mal·e·fac·tor /málifaktər/ *n.* a criminal; an evildoer.

ma·lef·ic /məléfik/ *adj. literary* (of magical arts, etc.) harmful; baleful.

ma·lef·i·cent /məléfisənt/ *adj. literary* **1** (often foll. by *to*) hurtful. **2** criminal. □□ **ma·lef·i·cence** /-səns/ *n.*

ma·lev·o·lent /məlévələnt/ *adj.* wishing evil to others. □□ **ma·lev·o·lence** /-ləns/ *n.* **ma·lev·o·lent·ly** *adv.*

mal·fea·sance /malféezəns/ *n. Law* evildoing. □□ **mal·fea·sant** /-zənt/ *n. & adj.*

mal·for·ma·tion /málformáyshən/ *n.* faulty formation. □□ **mal·formed** /-fáwrmd/ *adj.*

mal·func·tion /málfúngkshən/ *n. & v.* ● *n.* a failure

mal·le·a·ble /máleeəbəl/ *adj.* **1** (of metal, etc.) that can be shaped by hammering. **2** adaptable; pliable; flexible. □□ **mal·le·a·bil·i·ty** *n.* **mal·le·a·bly** *adv.*

mal·lee /málee/ *n. Austral.* **1** any of several types of eucalyptus, esp. *Eucalyptus dumosa*, that flourish in arid areas. **2** a scrub formed by mallee.

mal·le·o·lus /məléeələs/ *n.* (*pl.* **malleoli** /-lī/) *Anat.* a bone with the shape of a hammerhead, esp. each of those forming a projection on either side of the ankle.

mal·let /málit/ *n.* **1** ▶ a hammer, usu. of wood. **2** a long-handled wooden hammer for striking a croquet or polo ball. ▷ CROQUET, POLO STICK

MALLET

mal·le·us /máleeəs/ (*pl.* **mallei** /-lee-ī/) *Anat.* a small bone in the middle ear transmitting the vibrations of the tympanum to the incus.

mal·low /málō/ *n.* any plant of the genus *Malva*, with hairy leaves and pink or purple flowers.

malm /maam/ *n.* **1** a soft chalky rock. **2** a loamy soil produced by the disintegration of this rock. **3** a fine-quality brick made originally from malm, marl, or a similar chalky clay.

malm·sey /maámzee/ *n.* a strong sweet wine orig. from Greece, now chiefly from Madeira.

mal·nour·ished /málnərisht, -núr-/ *adj.* suffering from malnutrition. □□ **mal·nour·ish·ment** /-nərishmənt, -núr-/ *n.*

mal·nu·tri·tion /málnōōtríshən, -nyōō-/ *n.* a dietary condition resulting from the absence of foods necessary for health; insufficient nutrition.

mal·oc·clu·sion /maləklōōzhən/ *n. Dentistry* faulty contact of opposing teeth when the jaws are closed.

mal·o·dor·ous /malṓdərəs/ *adj.* having an unpleasant smell.

M

Title: ***Encarta World English Dictionary***
Publisher: **St. Martin's Press**
Most recent copyright: **1999**
No. of volumes: **1**
Weight: **6 lbs., 6 ozs.**
Price: **$50.00**

Type size (entry words / definitions): **9 pt / 6.5 pt**
Columns per page: **3**
Guide words per page: **2–shown on left and right**
Pronunciation keys: **every other page**
Method for accent marks: **after syllable**
Order of definitions: **frequency of use**
Illustrative examples: **yes**
Illustrative quotations: **yes**
Placement of etymologies: **after definitions**
Synonym studies: **yes**
Word history studies: **yes**
Usage studies: **yes**
Pictorial illustrations (number): **3,500**
Encyclopedic information: **in main body**

Special features:
- **Special paragraphs on world English, regional English, and cultural notes**
- **Proofreader's marks**
- **Periodic table of the elements**
- **Table of world currencies**

Lord May·or *n.* the mayor of the City of London and some other large British boroughs and cities, e.g. York

Lord of Hosts *n.* the Christian God

Lord of Mis·rule *n.* in Europe in the 15th and 16th centuries, somebody appointed to organize celebrations and sporting events, especially at Christmas

Lord of the Flies *n.* = **Beelzebub** [Literal translation of Hebrew *ba'al zeḇūḇ* (see BEELZEBUB)]

lor·do·sis /lawr dṓssiss/ (*plural* **-dos·es** /-dṓ sèez/) *n.* **1.** MED **CURVATURE OF BACK** an unusual inward curving of the spine in the lower part of the back, which may be medically significant **2.** ZOOL **ARCHING OF BACK DURING SEX** an inward arching of the back of female mammals during sexual stimulation [Early 18thC. Via modern Latin from Greek *lordōsis*, from *lordos* "bent backward."] —**lor·dot·ic** /lawr dóttik/ *adj.*

Lord Pro·tec·tor *n.* = **Protector**

lords-and-la·dies *n.* = **cuckoopint** (*takes a singular verb*) [Said to be because some plants have dark spadices (the "lords") and some light (the "ladies")]

Lord's Day *n.* the Christian Sabbath

lord·ship /láwrd shìp/ *n.* the position held by, land owned by, or period of tenure of, a lord (*formal*)

Lord·ship *n.* in the United Kingdom, a respectful way to refer to or address a judge, bishop, or some nobles

Lord's Prayer *n.* the most important prayer in Christianity, which Jesus Christ taught to his disciples according to the Gospels of Luke and Matthew

Lord's Sup·per *n.* = **Holy Communion** [So called because Holy Communion commemorates the LAST SUPPER of Jesus Christ and his disciples]

Lord's Ta·ble *n.* the altar or communion table in a Protestant church

lord·y /láwrdee/ *interj.* used to express surprise, shock, or disappointment (*dated informal*)

lore[1] /lawr/ *n.* **1.** **KNOWLEDGE HANDED DOWN VERBALLY** acquired knowledge or wisdom on a particular subject, e.g.,

Lorgnette

by the ancient Romans [Early 18thC. From Latin, literally "breastplate," formed from *lorum* "strap, thong."]

lor·i·keet /láwri kèet/ (*plural* **-keets** *or* **-keet**) *n.* a small brightly-colored long-necked parrot native to Australia and other Pacific Islands that has a bristle-tipped tongue for extracting nectar and pollen from flowers. Genera: *Trichoglosus* and *Glossopsitta.* [Late 18thC. Formed from LORY, modeled on *parakeet.*]

lo·ris /láwriss/ (*plural* **-ris**) *n.* a small slow-moving nocturnal tree-dwelling primate native to tropical regions of southern Asia that has large eyes, dense wooly fur, a vestigial index finger, and no tail [Late 18thC. From French, of uncertain origin: perhaps from obsolete Dutch *leoris* "clown, fool," ultimately from Latin *lurid* "pale" (source of English *lurid.*]

lorn /lawrn/ *adj.* forsaken or forlorn (*archaic literary*) [13thC. Past participle of *lese* "to lose," from Old English *-lēosan* (source of English *forlorn*).]

lor·ry /láwree/ (*plural* **-ries**) *n. U.K.* = **truck** [Mid-19thC. Origin uncertain: perhaps from the name *Laurie*; or from northern English dialect *lurry* "to haul," of unknown origin.]

lo·ry /láwree/ (*plural* **-ries** *or* **-ry**) *n.* a small brightly-colored parrot native to Australia and Indonesia that has a bristle-tipped tongue for extracting nectar and pollen from flowers. It has a heavier build than the lorikeet. Subfamily: Loriidae. [Late

to make somebody understand something ○ *You've lost me there.* **15.** *vti.* **RUN SLOW** to be or become slow by an amount of time (*refers to a timepiece*) [Old English *losian* "to perish, destroy, or lose," formed from *los* (see LOSS)] —**los·a·ble** *adj.* —**los·a·ble·ness** *n.* ◇ **lose it 1.** to become removed from reality (*informal*) **2.** to be unable to maintain emotional control or composure (*informal*)

lose out *vi.* to fail to win or obtain something in a competition or rivalry (*informal*)

los·er /lóozər/ *n.* **1.** **SOMEBODY WHO HAS NOT WON** a person or team that has failed to win a particular contest **2.** **SOMEBODY UNSUCCESSFUL OR UNLUCKY** somebody who is unsuccessful or unlucky and seems destined to fail repeatedly **3.** **SOCIAL MISFIT** somebody who is unable or unwilling to adjust to society (*informal insult*)

Losey /lṓzee/, **Joseph** (1909–84) U.S. movie director. His works explored social issues and criticized American society. In 1951 he was blacklisted as left wing and moved to Europe. Full name **Joseph Walton Losey**

Los Ga·tos /los gáttəss/ town in Santa Clara County, western California, situated 8 mi./13 km southwest of San Jose. Population: 27,357 (1990).

los·ings /lóozingz/ *npl.* money or possessions that are lost, especially through gambling

loss /lawss/ *n.* **1.** **FACT OF NO LONGER HAVING SOMETHING** the fact of no longer having something or of having less of something **2.** **SOMEBODY OR SOMETHING LOST** somebody or something that has been lost **3.** **DEATH** the death of somebody **4.** **MONEY SPENT IN EXCESS OF INCOME** the amount of money by which a company's or person's expenses exceed income or profit (*often used in the plural*) **5.** **SAD FEELING** a feeling of sadness, loneliness, or emptiness at the absence of somebody or something **6.** **REDUCTION** a reduction in the level of something, especially in the body ○ *weight loss* **7.** **INSTANCE OF LOSING CONTEST** an instance of losing a competition, race, or contest **8.** ELEC **DROP IN POWER CAUSED BY RESISTANCE** a drop in power caused by resistance in an electric circuit **9.** **INSTANCE OR AMOUNT OF CLAIM** an instance or the amount of a claim made by an insurance policyholder [Old English *los* "ruin,

Title: **Merriam-Webster's Collegiate® Dictionary, Tenth Edition**
Publisher: **Merriam-Webster, Inc.**
Most recent copyright: **1999**
No. of volumes: **1**
Weight: **4.5 lbs.**
Price: **$24.95**

Type size (entry words/definitions): **7 pt / 6.5 pt**
Columns per page: **2**
Guide words per page: **2–both shown together**
Pronunciation keys: **every other page**
Method for accent marks: **before syllable**
Order of definitions: **historical**
Illustrative examples: **yes**
Illustrative quotations: **yes**
Placement of etymologies: **before definitions**
Synonym studies: **yes**
Word history studies: **no**
Usage studies: **yes**
Pictorial illustrations (number): **700**
Encyclopedic information: **in separate sections**

Special features:
- **List of abbreviations and symbols**
- **Foreign words and phrases**
- **Guide to punctuation**
- **Forms of address**
- **Charts of geologic time, chemical elements**

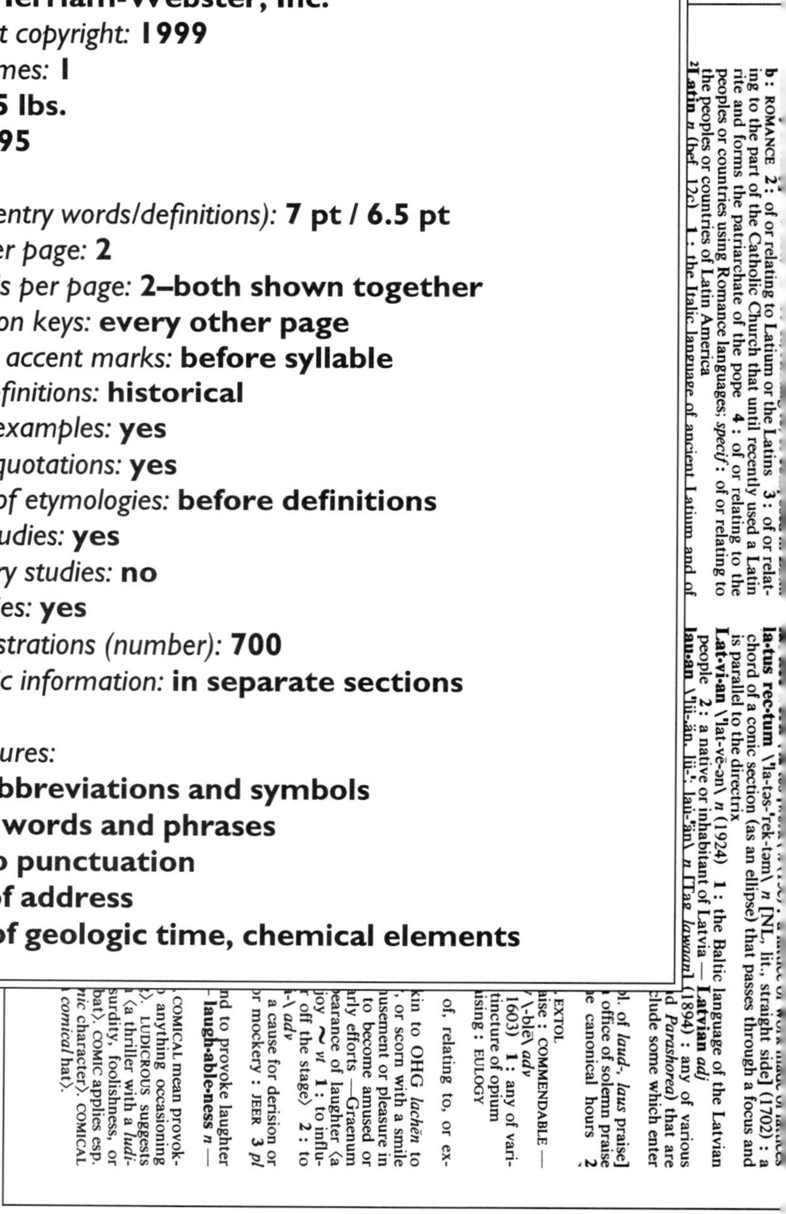
b : ROMANCE 2 : of or relating to Latium or the Latins 3 : of or relating to the part of the Catholic Church that until recently used a Latin rite and forms the patriarchate of the pope 4 : of or relating to the peoples or countries using Romance languages; *specif* : of or relating to the peoples or countries of Latin America
²Latin *n* (bef. 12c) 1 : the Italic language of ancient Latium and of

la·tus rec·tum \ˈlā-təs-ˈrek-təm\ *n* [NL, lit., straight side] (1702) : a chord of a conic section (as an ellipse) that passes through a focus and is parallel to the directrix
Lat·vi·an \ˈlat-vē-ən\ *n* (1924) 1 : the Baltic language of the Latvian people 2 : a native or inhabitant of Latvia — **Latvian** *adj*
lau·an \ˈlü-ˌän, lü-ˈ, lau-ˈän\ *n* [Tag *lawaan*] (1894) : any of various

658 lateralization • laughably

lat•er•al•i•za•tion \ˌla-tə-rə-lə-ˈzā-shən, ˌla-trə-\ *n* (ca. 1899) : localization of function or activity on one side of the body in preference to the other — **lat•er•al•ize** \ˈla-tə-rə-ˌlīz, ˈla-trə-\ *vt*
lateral line *n* (1870) : a canal along the side of a fish containing pores that open into tubes supplied with sense organs sensitive to low vibrations; *also* : one of these tubes or sense organs
lat•er•ite \ˈla-tə-ˌrīt\ *n* [L *later* brick] (1807) : a residual product of rock decay that is red in color and has a high content in the oxides of iron and hydroxide of aluminum — **lat•er•it•ic** \ˌla-tə-ˈri-tik\ *adj*
lat•er•i•za•tion \ˌla-tə-rə-ˈzā-shən\ *n* (ca. 1882) : the process of conversion of rock to laterite
[1]**lat•est** \ˈlā-təst\ *adj* (1588) **1** *archaic* : LAST **2** : most recent
[2]**latest** *n* (1884) **1** : the latest acceptable time — usu. used in the phrase *at the latest* **2** : something that is the most recent or currently fashionable ⟨the ~ in diving techniques⟩
late•wood \ˈlāt-ˌwu̇d\ *n* (ca. 1933) : SUMMERWOOD
la•tex \ˈlā-ˌteks\ *n, pl* **la•ti•ces** \ˈlā-tə-ˌsēz, ˈla-\ *or* **la•tex•es** [NL *latic-, latex,* fr. L, fluid] (1835) **1** : a milky usu. white fluid that is produced by cells of various seed plants (as of the milkweed, spurge, and poppy families) and is the source of rubber, gutta-percha, chicle, and balata **2** : a water emulsion of a synthetic rubber or plastic obtained by polymerization and used esp. in coatings (as paint) and adhesives
lath \ˈlath *also* ˈlath\ *n, pl* **laths** *or* **lath** [ME, fr. (assumed) OE *læthth-;* akin to OHG *latta* lath, W *llath* yard] (13c) **1** : a thin narrow strip of wood nailed to rafters, joists, or studding as a groundwork for slates, tiles, or plaster **2** : a building material in sheets used as a base for plaster **3** : a quantity of laths — **lath** *vt*
[1]**lathe** \ˈlāth\ *n* [prob. fr. ME *lath* supporting stand] (ca. 1611) : a machine in which work is rotated about a horizontal axis and shaped by a fixed tool
[2]**lathe** *vt* **lathed; lath•ing** (ca. 1903) : to cut or shape with a lathe
[1]**lath•er** \ˈla-thər\ *n* [(assumed) ME, fr. OE *lēathor;* akin to L *lavere* to wash — more at LYE] (bef. 12c) **1 a** : a foam or froth formed when a detergent (as soap) is agitated in water **b** : foam or froth from profuse sweating (as on a horse) **2** : an agitated or overwrought state : DITHER — **lath•ery** \-th(ə-)rē\ *adj*
[2]**lather** *vb* **lath•ered; lath•er•ing** \-th(ə-)riŋ\ *vt* (bef. 12c) **1** : to spread lather over **2** : to beat severely : FLOG ~ *vi* : to form a lather or a froth like lather — **lath•er•er** \-thər-ər\ *n*
lath•y•rism \ˈla-thə-ˌri-zəm\ *n* [NL *Lathyrus,* fr. Gk *lathyros,* a type of pea] (ca. 1888) : a diseased condition of humans, domestic animals, and esp. horses that results from poisoning by a substance found in some legumes (genus *Lathyrus* and esp. *L. sativus*) and is characterized esp. by spastic paralysis of the hind or lower limbs
lath•y•rit•ic \ˌla-thə-ˈri-tik\ *adj* (1960) : of, relating to, affected with, or characteristic of lathyrism ⟨~ rats⟩ ⟨~ cartilage⟩
latices *pl of* LATEX
la•tic•i•fer \lā-ˈti-sə-fər\ *n* [ISV *latici-* (fr. NL *latic-, latex*) + *-fer*] (ca. 1928) : a plant cell or vessel that contains latex
la•ti•fun•dio \ˌlä-tə-ˈfün-dē-ˌō\ *n, pl* **-di•os** [Sp, fr. L *latifundium*] (ca. 1902) : a latifundium in Spain or Latin America
lat•i•fun•di•um \ˌla-tə-ˈfən-dē-əm\ *n, pl* **-dia** \-dē-ə\ [L, fr. *latus* wide + *fundus* piece of landed property, foundation, bottom — more at BOTTOM] (1630) : a great landed estate with primitive agriculture and

lat•i•tude \ˈla-tə-ˌtüd, -ˌtyüd\ *n* [ME, fr. L *latitudin-, latitudo,* fr. *latus* wide; akin to OCS *postĭlati* to spread] (14c) **1** *archaic* : extent or distance from side to side : WIDTH **2** : angular distance from some specified circle or plane of reference: as **a** : angular distance north or south from the earth's equator measured through 90 degrees **b** : angular distance of a celestial body from the ecliptic **c** : a region or locality as marked by its latitude **3 a** *archaic* : SCOPE, RANGE **b** : the range of exposures within which a film or plate will produce a negative or positive of satisfactory quality **4** : freedom of action or choice — **lat•i•tu•di•nal** \ˌla-tə-ˈtüd-nəl, -ˈtyüd-; -ˈtü-dᵊn-əl, -ˈtyü-\ *adj* — **lat•i•tu•di•nal•ly** *adv*

latitude 2a: hemisphere marked with parallels of latitude

lat•i•tu•di•nar•i•an \ˌla-tə-ˌtü-dᵊn-ˈer-ē-ən, -ˌtyü-\ *n* (1662) : a person who is broad and liberal in standards of religious belief and conduct — **latitudinarian** *adj* — **lat•i•tu•di•nar•i•an•ism** \-ē-ə-ˌni-zəm\ *n*
lat•ke \ˈlät-kə\ *n* [Yiddish, pancake, fr. Ukrainian *oladka*] (1927) : POTATO PANCAKE
lat•o•sol \ˈla-tə-ˌsȯl\ *n* [irreg. fr. L *later* brick + E *-sol* (as in *podsol,* var. of *podzol*)] (1949) : a leached red and yellow tropical soil — **lat•o•sol•ic** \ˌla-tə-ˈsȯ-lik\ *adj*
la•trine \lə-ˈtrēn\ *n* [F, fr. L *latrina,* contr. of *lavatrina,* fr. *lavare* to wash — more at LYE] (1642) **1** : a receptacle (as a pit in the earth) for use as a toilet **2** : TOILET
-latry *n comb form* [ME *-latrie,* fr. OF, fr. LL *-latria,* fr. Gk, fr. *latreia;* akin to Gk *latron* pay] : worship ⟨helio*latry*⟩
lat•te \ˈlä-(ˌ)tā\ *n* (1991) : CAFFE LATTE
lat•ten \ˈla-tᵊn\ *n* [ME *laton,* fr. MF] (14c) : a yellow alloy identical to or resembling brass typically hammered into thin sheets and formerly much used for church utensils
lat•ter \ˈla-tər\ *adj* [ME, fr. OE *lætra,* compar. of *læt* late] (bef. 12c) **1 a** : belonging to a subsequent time or period : more recent ⟨the ~ stages of growth⟩ **b** : of or relating to the end ⟨in their ~ days⟩ **c** : RECENT, PRESENT ⟨affected by ~ calamities⟩ **2** : of, relating to, or being the second of two groups or things or the last of several groups or things referred to ⟨of ham and beef the ~ meat is cheaper today⟩ ⟨of ham and beef the ~ is cheaper today⟩
lat•ter–day \ˈla-tər-ˌdā\ *adj* (1850) **1** : of present or recent times ⟨~ prophets⟩ **2** : of a later or subsequent time
Latter–day Saint *n, often cap D* (1834) : a member of any of several religious bodies tracing their origin to Joseph Smith in 1830 and accepting the Book of Mormon as divine revelation : MORMON
lat•ter•ly *adv* (1734) **1** : LATER **2** : of late : RECENTLY
lat•tice \ˈla-təs\ *n* [ME *latis,* fr. MF *lattis*] (14c) **1 a** : a framework or structure of crossed wood or metal strips **b** : a window, door, or gate having a lattice **c** : a network or design resembling a lattice **2** : a regular geometrical arrangement of points or objects over an area or in space; *specif* : the arrangement of atoms in a crystal **3** : a mathematical set that has some elements ordered and that is such that for any two elements there exists a greatest element in the subset of all elements less

Title: **The Oxford American Dictionary and Language Guide**
Publisher: **Oxford University Press**
Most recent copyright: **2000**
No. of volumes: **1**
Weight: **5 lbs.**
Price: **$30.00**

Type size (entry words / definitions): **7 pt / 7 pt**
Columns per page: **2**
Guide words per page: **2–both shown together**
Pronunciation keys: **front only**
Method for accent marks: **above vowel**
Order of definitions: **frequency of use**
Illustrative examples: **yes**
Illustrative quotations: **no**
Placement of etymologies: **after definitions**
Synonym studies: **yes**
Word history studies: **yes**
Usage studies: **yes**
Pictorial illustrations (number): **600**
Encyclopedic information: **in separate sections**

Special features:

- **Pronunciation, punctuation, and spelling tips**
- **Tables of weights and measures, signs and symbols, chemical elements**
- **Proofreaders' marks**
- **Chronologies of U.S. and world history**
- **Maps of world nations**

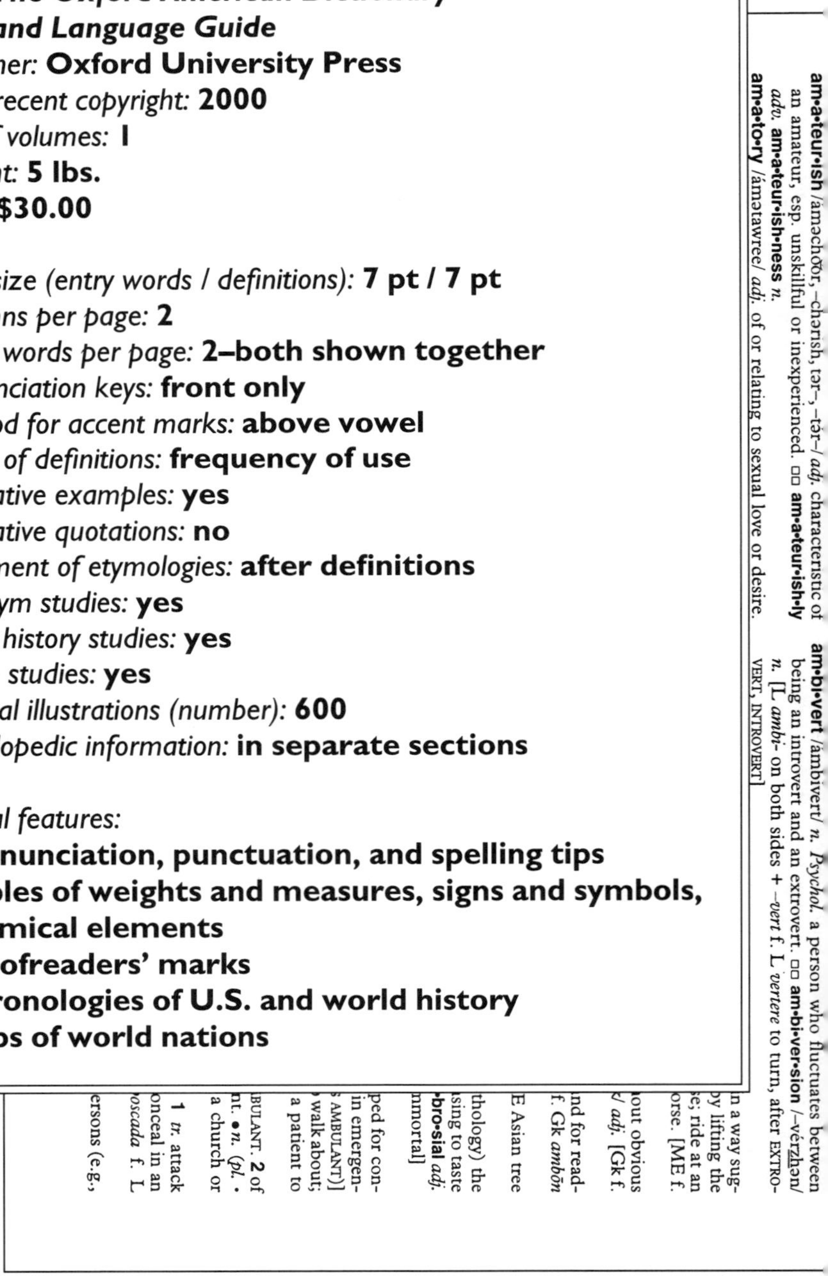
am•a•teur•ish /ámәchŏor, –chәrish, tәr–, –tәr–/ *adj.* characteristic of an amateur, esp. unskillful or inexperienced. □□ **am•a•teur•ish•ly** *adv.* **am•a•teur•ish•ness** *n.*

am•a•to•ry /ámәtawree/ *adj.* of or relating to sexual love or desire.

am•bi•vert /ámbivert/ *n. Psychol.* a person who fluctuates between being an introvert and an extrovert. □□ **am•bi•ver•sion** /–vérzhәn/ *n.* [L *ambi-* on both sides + *–vert* f. L *vertere* to turn, after EXTROVERT, INTROVERT]

AM ~ ambush **28**

AM *abbr.* **1** amplitude modulation. **2** Master of Arts. **3** Member of the Order of Australia. [(sense 2) L *artium Magister*]
Am *symb. Chem.* the element americium.
am *1st person sing. present* of BE.
a.m. *abbr.* (also **A.M.** or **AM**) between midnight and noon. [L *ante meridiem*]
AMA *abbr.* American Medical Association.
am•a•dou /ámədōō/ *n.* a spongy and combustible tinder prepared from dry fungi. [F f. mod.Prov., lit. = lover (because quickly kindled) f. L (as AMATEUR)]
a•mah /aámə, aámaa/ *n.* (in Asia) a nursemaid or maid. [Port. *ama* nurse]
a•mal•gam /əmálgəm/ *n.* **1** a mixture or blend. **2** an alloy of mercury with one or more other metals, used esp. in dentistry. [ME f. F *amalgame* or med.L *amalgama* f. Gk *malagma* an emollient]
a•mal•ga•mate /əmálgəmayt/ *v.* **1** *tr. & intr.* combine or unite to form one structure, organization, etc. **2** *tr.* (of metals) alloy with mercury. □□ **a•mal•ga•ma•tion** /–máyshən/ *n.* [med.L *amalgamare amalgamat-* (as AMALGAM)]
a•man•u•en•sis /əmányōō-énsis/ *n.* (*pl.* **amanuenses** /–seez/) **1** a person who writes from dictation or copies manuscripts. **2** a literary assistant. [L f. (*servus*) *a manu* secretary + *–ensis* belonging to]
am•a•ranth /ámərənth/ *n.* **1** any plant of the genus *Amaranthus*, usu. having small green, red, or purple tinted flowers, e.g., prince's feather and pigweed. **2** an imaginary flower that never fades. **3** a purple color. □□ **am•a•ran•thine** /–əránthin, –thīn/ *adj.* [F *amarante* or mod.L *amaranthus* f. L f. Gk *amarantos* everlasting f. *a-* not + *marainō* wither, alt. after *polyanthus*, etc.]
am•a•ret•to /amərétō/ *n.* an almond-flavored liqueur. [It. dimin. of *amaro* bitter f. L *amarus*]
am•a•ryl•lis /ámərílis/ *n.* **1** a plant genus with a single species, *Amaryllis belladonna*, a bulbous lilylike plant native to S. Africa with white, pink, or red flowers (also called **belladonna lily**). **2** any of various related plants formerly of this genus now transferred to other genera, notably *Hippeastrum*. [L f. Gk *Amarullis*, name of a country girl]
a•mass /əmás/ *v.tr.* **1** gather or heap together. **2** accumulate (esp. riches). □□ **a•mass•er** *n.* **a•mass•ment** *n.* [F *amasser* or med.L *amassare* ult. f. L *massa* MASS[1]]
am•a•teur /áməchoor, –chər, –tər, –tór/ *n. & adj.* • *n.* **1 a** a person who engages in a pursuit (e.g., an art or sport) as a pastime rather than a profession. **b** *derog.* a person who does something unskillfully, in the manner of an amateur rather than a professional. **2** (foll.

tion of the intestine of the sperm whale, found floating in tropical seas and used in perfume manufacture. [ME f. OF *ambre gris* gray AMBER]
am•ber•jack /ámbərjak/ *n.* any large brightly-colored marine fish of the genus *Seriola* found in tropical and subtropical Atlantic waters.
am•bi•ance var. of AMBIENCE.
am•bi•dex•trous /ámbidékstrəs/ *adj.* (*Brit.* also **ambidexterous**) **1** able to use the right and left hands equally well. **2** working skillfully in more than one medium. □□ **am•bi•dex•ter•i•ty** /–stéritee/ *n.* **am•bi•dex•trous•ly** *adv.* **am•bi•dex•trous•ness** *n.* [LL *ambidexter* f. *ambi-* on both sides + *dexter* right-handed]
am•bi•ence /ámbeeəns, aaNbeeaáNs/ *n.* (also **am•bi•ance**) the surroundings or atmosphere of a place. [AMBIENT + –ENCE or F *ambiance*]

PRONUNCIATION TIP **ambience**

Although many English speakers pronounce this word in a manner reflective of its French origins (AHM-bee-ahns), the American pronunciation AM-bee-ens is also widely used. It is sometimes spelled *ambiance*.

am•bi•ent /ámbeeənt/ *adj.* surrounding. [F *ambiant* or L *ambiens –entis* pres. part. of *ambire* go round]
am•bi•gu•i•ty /ámbigyóoitee/ *n.* (*pl.* **•ties**) **1 a** a double meaning which is either deliberate or caused by inexactness of expression. **b** an example of this. **2** an expression able to be interpreted in more than one way (e.g., *fighting dogs should be avoided*). [ME f. OF *ambiguité* or L *ambiguitas* (as AMBIGUOUS)]
am•big•u•ous /ambígyōōəs/ *adj.* **1** having an obscure or double meaning. **2** difficult to classify. □□ **am•big•u•ous•ly** *adv.* **am•big•u•ous•ness** *n.* [L *ambiguus* doubtful f. *ambigere* f. *ambi-* both ways + *agere* drive]
am•bit /ámbit/ *n.* **1** the scope, extent, or bounds of something. **2** precincts or environs. [ME f. L *ambitus* circuit f. *ambire*: see AMBIENT]
am•bi•tion /ambíshən/ *n.* **1** (often foll. by *to* + infin.) the determination to achieve success or distinction, usu. in a chosen field. **2** the object of this determination. **3** energy; interest in activity, etc. **4** aggressive self-centeredness. [ME f. OF f. L *ambitio –onis* f. *ambire ambit-* canvass for votes: see AMBIENT]
am•bi•tious /ambíshəs/ *adj.* **1 a** full of ambition. **b** showing ambition (*an ambitious attempt*). **2** (foll. by *of*, or *to* + infin.) strongly determined. □□ **am•bi•tious•ly** *adv.* **am•bi•tious•ness** *n.* [ME f. OF *ambitieux* f. L *ambitiosus* (as AMBITION)]
am•biv•a•lence /ambívələns/ *n.* (also **ambivalency** /–lənsee/) **1** the

Title: **Random House Webster's College Dictionary**
Publisher: **Random House, Inc.**
Most recent copyright: **1999**
No. of volumes: **1**
Weight: **3 lbs., 13 ozs.**
Price: **$24.95**

Type size (entry words / definitions): **6.5 pt / 6.4 pt**
Columns per page: **2**
Guide words per page: **2–both shown together**
Pronunciation keys: **front only**
Method for accent marks: **after syllable**
Order of definitions: **frequency of use**
Illustrative examples: **yes**
Illustrative quotations: **no**
Placement of etymologies: **after definitions**
Synonym studies: **yes**
Word history studies: **no**
Usage studies: **yes**
Pictorial illustrations (number): **500**
Encyclopedic information: **in main body**

Special features:
- **Vocabulary alerts readers to "sensitive" words and usages**
- **Guide for writers**
- **Charts of signs and symbols, chemical elements, nations of the world, states of the U.S., presidents of the U.S., proofreaders' marks**
- **Maps of the world (8 pages)**

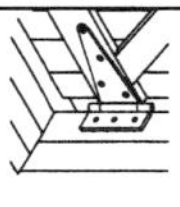
T hinge

Hil•des•heim (hil′des hīm′), *n.* a city in N central Germany. 106,095.

Hil•i•gay•non (hil′i gī′nən), *n., pl.* **-nons,** (*esp. collectively*) **-non. 1.** a member of a people of the central Philippines, living mainly on Panay and W Negros. **2.** the Austronesian language of the Hiligaynons.

hill (hil), *n., v.,* **hilled, hill•ing.** **—***n.* **1.** a natural elevation of the earth's surface, smaller than a mountain. **2.** an incline, esp. in a road. **3.** an artificial heap, pile, or mound. **4. a.** a mound of earth raised about and above a plant or plant cluster. **b.** a cluster of plants within such a mound. **5. the Hill,** CAPITOL HILL. **—***v.t.* **6.** to surround with hills. **7.** to form into a hill or heap. **—*Idiom.* 8. over the hill,** advanced in age; past one's prime. [bef. 1000; ME; OE *hyll,* c. MD *hille;* akin to Go *hallus* rock, L *collis* hill] **—hill′er,** *n.*

Hill (hil), *n.* **1. James Jerome,** 1838–1916, U.S. railroad builder and financier, born in Canada. **2. Joe,** 1879–1915, U.S. labor organizer and songwriter, born in Sweden.

Hil•la•ry (hil′ə rē), *n.* **Sir Edmund P.,** born 1919, New Zealand mountain climber who scaled Mount Everest 1953.

hill•bil•ly (hil′bil′ē), *n., pl.* **-lies,** *adj.* **—Usage.** This term is usually used with disparaging intent, implying that a person who lives far away from a town or city lacks culture or education. However, the term is sometimes used in a humorous way without intent to offend. **—***n.* **1.** *Older Slang: Usu. Disparaging.* (a term used to refer to a person from a backwoods or other remote area, esp. from the mountains of the southern U.S.) **—***adj.* **2.** of, like, or pertaining to hillbillies: *hillbilly humor.* [1895–1900, *Amer.*; HILL + *Billy,* familiar form of *William*]

hill′billy mu′sic, *n.* COUNTRY MUSIC. [1950–55]

Hil•lel (hil′el, -āl, hi lāl′), *n.* c60 B.C.–A.D. 9?, Palestinian rabbi and interpreter of Biblical law.

Hil•ling•don (hil′ing dən), *n.* a borough of Greater London, England. 232,200.

hill′ my′na, *n.* a myna of S and SE Asia, *Gracula religiosa,* having glossy black plumage and yellow neck wattles: bred in captivity for its ability to mimic speech. [1885–90]

hill•ock (hil′ək), *n.* a small hill. [1350–1400] **—hill′ocked, hill′ock•y,** *adj.*

Hill′ of Tar′a, *n.* See under TARA.

hill•side (hil′sīd′), *n.* the side or slope of a hill. [1350–1400]

hill•top (hil′top′), *n.* the top or summit of a hill. [1375–1425]

hill•y (hil′ē), *adj.,* **hill•i•er, hill•i•est. 1.** full of hills; having many hills. **2.** resembling a hill; elevated; steep. [1350–1400] **—hill′i•ness,** *n.*

Hi•lo (hē′lō), *n.* a seaport on E Hawaii island, in SE Hawaii. 35,269.

hilt (hilt), **—***n.* **1.** the handle of a sword or dagger. **2.** the handle of any weapon or tool. **—***v.t.* **3.** to furnish with a hilt. **—*Idiom.* 4. to the hilt,** to the maximum extent or degree; completely; fully. [bef. 900; ME, OE *hilt(e),* c. OS *hilte, helta,* OHG *helza,* ON *hjalt*]

hin (hin), *n.* an ancient Hebrew unit of liquid measure equal to about 1½ gallons (5.7 liters). [1350–1400; ME < LL < Gk < Heb *hīn* < Egyptian *hnw* a liquid measure, lit., jar]

Hi•na•ya•na (hē′nə yä′nə), *n.* THERAVADA. [1865–70; < Skt, = *hīna* lesser, inferior + *yāna* vehicle] **—Hi′na•ya′nist,** *n.*

hind[1] (hīnd), *adj.* situated in the rear or at the back; posterior: *the hind legs of an animal.* [1300–50; ME *hinde;* cf. OE *hindan* (adv.) from behind, at the back, c. OHG *hintana,* Go *hindana;* cf. BEHIND, HINDER[2]] **—Syn.** See BACK[1].

hind[2] (hīnd), *n., pl.* **hinds,** (*esp. collectively*) **hind. 1.** the female of the European red deer in and after the third year. **2.** any of various groupers of the genus *Epinephelus,* of warm Atlantic seas, as the orange-speckled *E. adscensionis* **(rock hind).** [bef. 900; ME, OE, c. MD *hinde,* OHG *hinta*]

hind[3] (hīnd), *n.* **1.** a peasant; rustic. **2.** *Chiefly Scot.* a farm laborer. [bef. 1000; alter. of ME *hine* (pl.) servants, OE (Anglian) *hīne, hī(g)na,* gen. of *hīgan* (West Saxon *hīwan*) members of a household; cf. HIDE[3]]

Hind., **1.** Hindu. **2.** Hindustan.

hind•brain (hīnd′brān′), *n.* the most posterior of the three embryonic divisions of the vertebrate brain or the parts derived from this tissue, including the medulla oblongata, the pons of mammals, and the cerebellum; rhombencephalon. [1885–90]

Hin•de•mith (hin′də mith, -mit), *n.* **Paul,** 1895–1963, U.S. composer, born in Germany.

Hin•den•burg (hin′dən bûrg′), *n.* **Paul von** (*Paul von Beneckendorff und von Hindenburg*), 1847–1934, German field marshal; 2nd president of Germany 1925–34.

hin•der[1] (hin′dər), **—***v.t.* **1.** to cause delay, interruption, or difficulty in; hamper; impede. **2.** to prevent from doing, acting, or happening; stop. **—***v.i.* **3.** to be an obstacle or impediment. [bef. 1000; ME *hindren,* OE *hindrian* to hold back] **—Syn.** See PREVENT.

hind•er[2] (hīn′dər), *adj.* situated at the rear or back; posterior. [1250–1300; ME; cf. OE *hinder* behind, c. OS *hindiro,* OHG *hintar,* Go *hindar*]

hind•gut (hīnd′gut′), *n.* **1. a.** the last portion of the vertebrate alimentary canal, between the cecum and the anus. **b.** the posterior part of the digestive tract of arthropods. **2.** the posterior part of the embryonic vertebrate alimentary canal, from which the colon develops. Compare FOREGUT, MIDGUT. [1875–80]

Hin•di (hin′dē), *n.* an Indo-Aryan language of N India, having equal status with English as an official language throughout India. [1790–1800; < Hindi, Urdu *Hindī* = Pers *Hind* India (cf. Skt *Sindhu* the river Indus; sense extended to "region of the Indus, SIND") + *-ī* suffix]

hind•most (hīnd′mōst′), *adj.* farthest behind or nearest the rear; last.

Hin•doo•ism (hin′do͞o iz′əm), *n.* HINDUISM.

hind•quar•ter (hīnd′kwôr′tər, -kwô′-), *n.* **1. hindquarters,** the rear [illegible]

Title: ***Webster's American Family Dictionary***
Publisher: **Random House, Inc.**
Most recent copyright: **1999**
No. of volumes: **1**
Weight: **3 lbs., 8 ozs.**
Price: **$23.95**

Type size (entry words / definitions): **6.8 pt / 6.5 pt**
Columns per page: **2**
Guide words per page: **2–both shown together**
Pronunciation keys: **front only**
Method for accent marks: **after syllable**
Order of definitions: **frequency of use**
Illustrative examples: **yes**
Illustrative quotations: **no**
Placement of etymologies: **after definitions (few)**
Synonym studies: **no**
Word history studies: **no**
Usage studies: **yes**
Pictorial illustrations (number): **300**
Encyclopedic information: **in main body**

Special features:

- **Vocabulary excludes obscene and offensive words**
- **Vocabulary includes important terms from the Bible, American history, and American civics**
- **Guide for writers**
- **Charts of signs and symbols, chemical elements, nations of the world, U.S. presidents and vice-presidents, proofreaders' marks**
- **Declaration of Independence, Gettysburg Address, Sermon on the Mount**

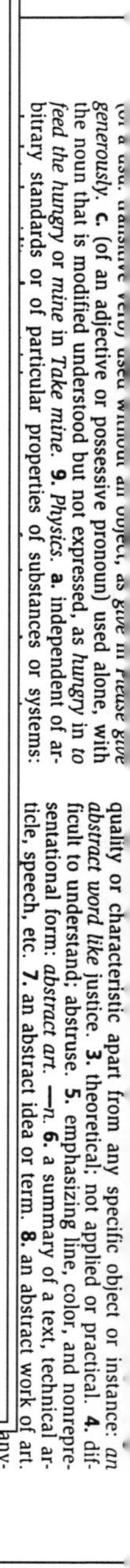
generously. **c.** (of an adjective or possessive pronoun) used alone, with the noun that is modified understood but not expressed, as *hungry* in *to feed the hungry* or *mine* in *Take mine.* **9.** *Physics.* **a.** independent of arbitrary standards or of particular properties of substances or systems:

quality or characteristic apart from any specific object or instance: *an abstract word like* justice. **3.** theoretical; not applied or practical. **4.** difficult to understand; abstruse. **5.** emphasizing line, color, and nonrepresentational form: *abstract art.* —*n.* **6.** a summary of a text, technical article, speech, etc. **7.** an abstract idea or term. **8.** an abstract work of art.

ABS to **Abu Dhabi** 2

ABS, antilock braking system.
abs., **1.** absent. **2.** absolute. **3.** abstract.
Ab•sa•lom (ab′sə ləm), *n.* the third son of David: he rebelled against his father and was slain by Joab. II Sam. 13–18.
ab•scess (ab′ses), *n.* a localized accumulation of pus in a body tissue. **—ab′scessed,** *adj.*
ab•scis•sa (ab sis′ə), *n., pl.* **-scis•sas, -scis•sae** (-sis′ē). (in plane Cartesian coordinates) the x-coordinate of a point: its distance from the y-axis measured parallel to the x-axis. Compare ORDINATE.
ab•scis•sion (ab sizh′ən, -sish′-), *n.* **1.** the act of cutting off; sudden termination. **2.** the normal separation of flowers, fruit, and leaves from plants.
ab•scond (ab skond′), *v.i.* to depart in a sudden and secret manner, esp. to avoid capture and legal prosecution. **—ab•scond′ence,** *n.* **—ab•scond′er,** *n.*
ab•sence (ab′səns), *n.* **1.** the state of being away or not being present. **2.** a period of being away: *an absence of several weeks.* **3.** failure to attend or appear when expected. **4.** lack; deficiency: *the absence of proof.* **5.** inattentiveness; preoccupation; absent-mindedness: *absence of mind.*
ab•sent (*adj., prep.* ab′sənt; *v.* ab sent′, ab′sənt), *adj.* **1.** not in a certain place at a given time; away; missing; not present: *absent from class.* **2.** lacking; nonexistent: *Revenge was absent from his mind.* **3.** not attentive; preoccupied; absent-minded: *an absent expression.* **—*v.t.*** **4.** to take or keep (oneself) away: *to absent oneself from a meeting.* **—*prep.*** **5.** in the absence of; without. **—ab′sen•ta′tion,** *n.* **—ab•sent′er,** *n.*
ab•sen•tee (ab′sən tē′), *n.* **1.** a person who is absent, esp. from work or school. **2.** a person who absents himself or herself, as a property owner who does not live on or near certain property owned.
ab′sentee bal′lot, *n.* the ballot used for an absentee vote.
ab•sen•tee•ism (ab′sən tē′iz əm), *n.* frequent or habitual absence from work, school, etc.
ab′sentee vote′, *n.* a vote cast by a person who, because of absence from the usual voting district, illness, etc., has been permitted to vote by mail. **—ab′sentee vot′er,** *n.*
ab′sent-mind′ed or **ab′sent•mind′ed,** *adj.* preoccupied with one's thoughts so as to be unaware or forgetful of other matters. **—ab′sent-mind′ed•ly,** *adv.* **—ab′sent-mind′ed•ness,** *n.*
ab′sent without′ leave′, *adj., adv.* See AWOL.
ab•sinthe or **ab•sinth** (ab′sinth), *n.* a strong green liqueur made with wormwood and other herbs, having a bitter licorice flavor: now banned in most Western countries.
ab•so•lute (ab′sə lo͞ot′, ab′sə lo͞ot′), *adj.* **1.** being fully or perfectly as indicated; complete; perfect. **2.** free from restriction, limitation, or exception: *absolute power; absolute freedom.* **3.** outright; unqualified: *an absolute lie; an absolute denial.* **4.** unrestrained in the exercise of governmental power; not limited by laws or a constitution: *an absolute monarchy.* **5.** viewed independently; not comparative or relative; ulti-

being absolved. **2.** a remission of sin or of the punishment for sin, esp. as effected by a priest or bishop in the sacrament of penance. **—ab•sol′u•to′ry** (-sol′yə tôr′ē, -tōr′ē), *adj.*
ab•so•lut•ism (ab′sə lo͞o tiz′əm), *n.* **1.** the principle or the exercise of unrestricted power in government. **2.** any theory holding that values, principles, etc., are absolute and not relative, dependent, or changeable. **—ab′so•lut′ist,** *n., adj.* **—ab′so•lu•tis′tic,** *adj.*
ab•solve (ab zolv′, -solv′), *v.t.,* **-solved, solv•ing.** **1.** to free from guilt or blame or their consequences. **2.** to set free or release from some duty, obligation, or responsibility (usu. fol. by *from*). **3.** to grant pardon for; excuse. **4. a.** to grant or pronounce remission of sins to. **b.** to remit (a sin) by absolution. **—ab•solv′a•ble,** *adj.* **—ab•solv′er,** *n.*
ab•sorb (ab sôrb′, -zôrb′), *v.t.* **1.** to suck up or drink in (a liquid); soak up: *A sponge absorbs water.* **2.** to take in and assimilate; incorporate: *The empire absorbed many nations.* **3.** to involve the full attention of; engross: *This book will absorb the serious reader.* **4.** to occupy or fill (time, attention, etc.). **5.** to assimilate by chemical or molecular action. **6.** to take in without echo, recoil, or reflection: *to absorb shock; to absorb sound.* **7.** to take in and utilize: *to absorb information.* **8.** to pay for (costs, taxes, etc.). **—ab•sorb′a•ble,** *adj.* **—ab•sorb′a•bil′i•ty,** *n.*
ab•sorbed (ab sôrbd′, -zôrbd′), *adj.* deeply interested or involved; engrossed. **—ab•sorb′ed•ly,** *adv.* **—ab•sorb′ed•ness,** *n.*
ab•sorb•ent (ab sôr′bənt, -zôr′-), *adj.* **1.** capable of absorbing heat, light, moisture, etc.; tending to absorb. **—*n.*** **2.** a substance that absorbs. **—ab•sorb′en•cy,** *n.*
ab•sorb•ing (ab sôr′bing, -zôr′-), *adj.* extremely interesting or involving; engrossing. **—ab•sorb′ing•ly,** *adv.*
ab•sorp•tion (ab sôrp′shən, -zôrp′-), *n.* **1.** the act of absorbing. **2.** the state or process of being absorbed. **3.** assimilation. **4.** complete involvement or preoccupation. **5.** assimilation by molecular or chemical action. **6.** the removal of energy or particles from a beam by the medium through which the beam propagates. **—ab•sorp′tive,** *adj., n.*
ab•stain (ab stān′), *v.i.* **1.** to refrain voluntarily, esp. from something regarded as improper or unhealthy (usu. fol. by *from*): *to abstain from eating meat.* **2.** to refrain from casting one's vote: *a referendum in which two delegates abstained.*
ab•ste•mi•ous (ab stē′mē əs), *adj.* **1.** sparing or moderate in eating and drinking; temperate. **2.** characterized by abstinence. **3.** sparing: *an abstemious diet.* **—ab•ste′mi•ous•ly,** *adv.* **—ab•ste′mi•ous•ness,** *n.*
ab•sten•tion (ab sten′shən), *n.* **1.** an act or instance of abstaining. **2.** the withholding of one's vote.
ab•ster•gent (ab stûr′jənt), *adj.* **1.** cleansing. **2.** purgative. **—*n.*** **3.** a cleansing agent, as a detergent.
ab•sti•nence (ab′stə nəns) also **ab′sti•nen•cy,** *n.* **1.** forbearance from indulgence of an appetite. **2.** abstention from a drug, as alcohol or heroin, esp. a drug on which one is dependent: *total abstinence.* **3.** any self-restraint, self-denial, or forbearance. **4.** the refraining from certain

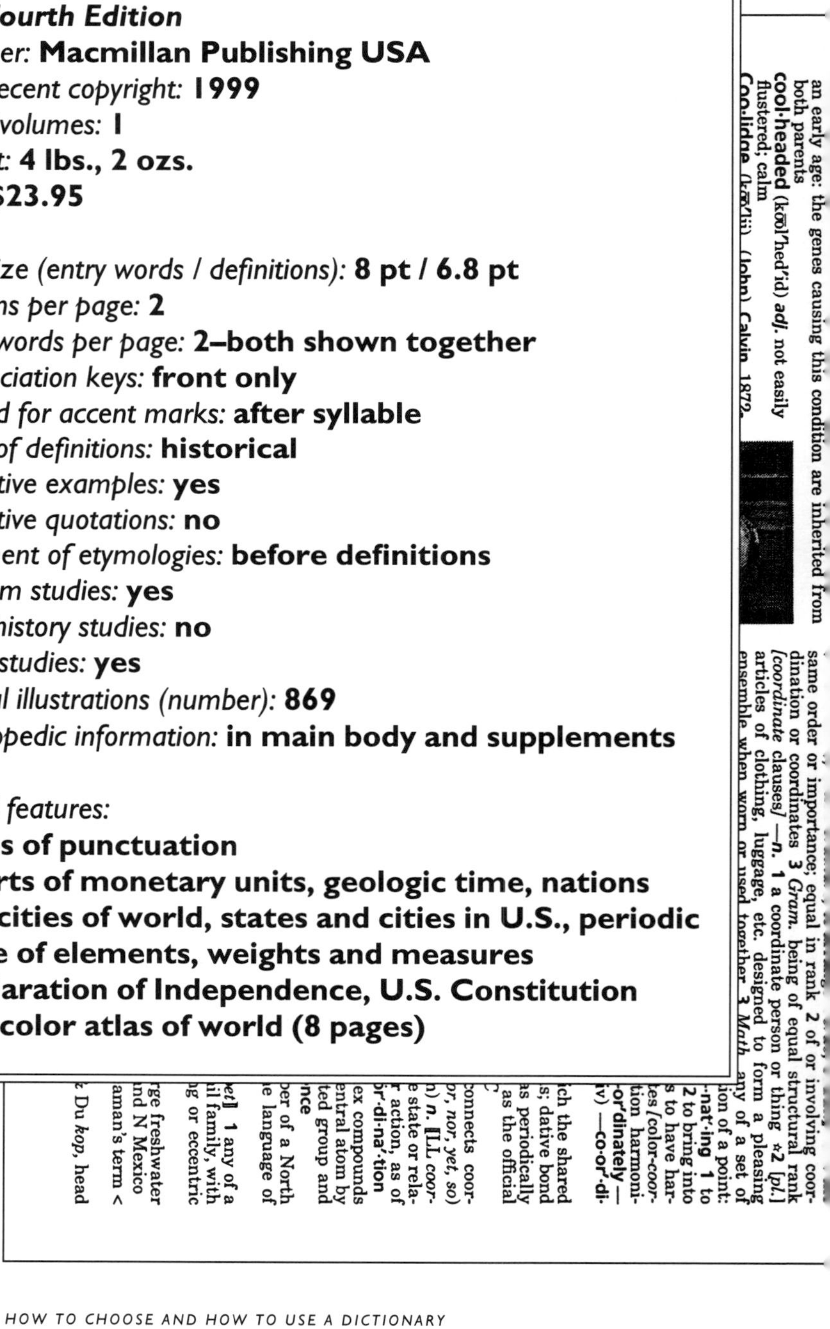

Title: **Webster's New World College Dictionary, Fourth Edition**
Publisher: **Macmillan Publishing USA**
Most recent copyright: **1999**
No. of volumes: **1**
Weight: **4 lbs., 2 ozs.**
Price: **$23.95**

Type size (entry words / definitions): **8 pt / 6.8 pt**
Columns per page: **2**
Guide words per page: **2–both shown together**
Pronunciation keys: **front only**
Method for accent marks: **after syllable**
Order of definitions: **historical**
Illustrative examples: **yes**
Illustrative quotations: **no**
Placement of etymologies: **before definitions**
Synonym studies: **yes**
Word history studies: **no**
Usage studies: **yes**
Pictorial illustrations (number): **869**
Encyclopedic information: **in main body and supplements**

Special features:
- **Rules of punctuation**
- **Charts of monetary units, geologic time, nations and cities of world, states and cities in U.S., periodic table of elements, weights and measures**
- **Declaration of Independence, U.S. Constitution**
- **Full-color atlas of world (8 pages)**

Cook Strait / cop — 320

Cook Strait strait between North Island & South Island, New Zealand: narrowest point, 16 mi (26 km)

cook·top (kook'tăp') ***n.*** **1** the upper surface of a kitchen stove, containing the burners or heating elements **2** such a surface or unit with heating elements installed separately, as on a kitchen counter

☆**cook·ware** (kook'wer') ***n.*** cooking utensils; pots, pans, etc.

cooky (kook'ē) ***n.***, *pl.* **cook'·ies** COOKIE

cool (kōōl) ***adj.*** ⟦ME & OE *col* < IE base **gel-*, cold, to freeze > CHILL, COLD, L *gelu*⟧ **1** moderately cold; neither warm nor very cold **2** tending to reduce discomfort in warm or hot weather *[cool clothes]* **3** *a)* not excited; calm; composed *[cool in an emergency]* ☆*b)* marked by control of the emotions; restrained *[cool jazz]* *c)* [Slang] emotionally uninvolved; uncommitted; dispassionate **4** showing dislike or indifference; not cordial *[a cool manner]* **5** calmly impudent or bold **6** not suggesting warmth: said of colors in the blue-green end of the spectrum **7** [Informal] without exaggeration *[he won a cool thousand dollars]* ☆**8** [Slang] very good, pleasing, etc.; excellent —***adv.*** in a cool manner —***n.*** **1** a cool place, time, thing, part, etc. *[the cool of the evening]* ☆**2** [Slang] cool, dispassionate attitude or manner —***vi.*** ⟦ME *colien* < OE *colian*, to cool⟧ to become cool or colder —***vt.*** to make cool or colder —**cool down** **1** to lower the body temperature, pulse, etc. after vigorous exercise **2** to become less heated, passionate, agitated, angry, etc. —☆**cool it** [Slang] to calm down —**cool off** **1** to calm down **2** to lose enthusiasm, interest, etc. —☆**cool out** [Slang] to make or become relaxed, calm, mollified, etc. *[soothing words cooled him out]* —☆**play it cool** [Slang] to exercise strict control over one's emotions; stay aloof, unenthusiastic, or uncommitted —**cool'·ish** ***adj.*** —**cool'ly** ***adv.*** —**cool'·ness** ***n.***

SYN.—**cool**, in this comparison, implies freedom from the heat of emotion or excitement, suggesting a calm, dispassionate attitude or a controlled alertness in difficult circumstances; **composed** suggests readiness to meet a trying situation through self-possession or the disciplining of one's emotions; **collected** stresses a being in full command of one's faculties or emotions in a distracting situation; **unruffled** suggests the maintenance of poise or composure in the face of something that might agitate or embarrass one; **nonchalant** stresses a cool lack of concern or casual indifference —***ANT.*** **excited, agitated**

cool·ant (kōōl'ənt) ***n.*** a substance, usually a fluid, used to remove heat, as from a nuclear reactor, an internal-combustion engine, molten metal, etc.: cf. REFRIGERANT

cool-down (kōōl'doun') ***n.*** the act or an instance of gradually slowing or cooling down after vigorous exercise

cooler (kōōl'ər) ***n.*** **1** a device, container, or room for cooling things or keeping them cool **2** anything that cools **3** a cold, refreshing

usually with *up* —☆***vi.*** [Slang] to sleep while on duty: said of a police officer —☆**fly the coop** [Slang] to escape, as from a jail

co-op[1] (kō'äp', kō äp') ***n.*** [Informal] a cooperative

co-op[2] or **coop** *abbrev.* cooperative

cooper (kōōp'ər) ***n.*** ⟦ME *couper* < MDu *cuper* < LL *cuparius* < L *cupa*, a cask: see COOP⟧ a person whose work is making or repairing barrels and casks —***vt., vi.*** to make or repair (barrels and casks)

Cooper (kōōp'ər) **1 Gary** (born *Frank James Cooper*) 1901-61; U.S. film actor **2 James Feni·more** (fen'ə môr') 1789-1851; U.S. novelist **3 Peter** 1791-1883; U.S. inventor, industrialist, & philanthropist

GARY COOPER

coop·er·age (-ij) ***n.*** **1** the workshop of a cooper **2** *a)* the work of a cooper *b)* the price charged for such work

co·oper·ate or **co-operate** (kō äp'ər āt') ***vi.*** **-·at'ed, -·at'·ing** ⟦< LL *cooperatus*, pp. of *cooperari*, to work together < L *co-*, with + *operari*, to work < *opus* (gen. *operis*), work: see OPUS⟧ **1** to act or work together with another or others for a common purpose **2** to combine so as to produce an effect **3** to engage in economic cooperation Also **co·öp'·er·ate'** —**co·op'era'·tor** ***n.*** or **co-op'era'tor**

co·opera·tion or **co-operation** (kō äp'ər ā'shən) ***n.*** ⟦LL *cooperatio*⟧ **1** the act of cooperating; joint effort or operation **2** the association of a number of people in an enterprise for mutual benefits or profits **3** *Ecol.* an interaction between organisms that is largely beneficial to all those participating Also **co·öp'·era'·tion** —**co·op'era'·tion·ist** ***n.*** or **co-op'era'tionist**

co·opera·tive or **co-operative** (kō äp'ər ə tiv, -ər āt'iv) ***adj.*** **1** cooperating or inclined to cooperate **2** designating or of an organization (as for the production or marketing of goods), an apartment house, store, etc. owned by and operated for the benefit of members who use its facilities or services —***n.*** a cooperative society, store, etc. Also **co·öp'·era·tive** —**co·op'era·tively** ***adv.*** or **co-op'eratively** —**co·op'era·tive·ness** ***n.*** or **co-op'erativeness**

☆**Coop·er's hawk** (kōōp'ərz) ⟦after Wm. *Cooper*, 19th-c. U.S. ornithologist⟧ a medium-sized hawk (*Accipiter cooperii*) with a long, rounded tail and short, rounded wings

coop·ery (kōōp'ər ē) ***n.***, *pl.* **-·er·ies** ⟦COOPER + -Y³⟧ the work, shop, or product of a cooper

co-opt (kō äpt', kō'äpt') ***vt.*** ⟦L *cooptare*, to choose, elect < *co-* (var. of *com-*), with + *optare*, to choose: see OPTION⟧ **1** to add (a person or persons) to a group by vote of those already members **2** to appoint as an associate **3** to persuade or lure (an opponent) to join one's own system, party, etc. **4** to make use of for one's own pur-

Title: **Webster's II New College Dictionary**
Publisher: **Houghton Mifflin Company**
Most recent copyright: **1999**
No. of volumes: **1**
Weight: **3 lbs., 8 ozs.**
Price: **$22.00**

Type size (entry words / definitions): **6.8 pt / 6.5 pt**
Columns per page: **2**
Guide words per page: **2–both shown together**
Pronunciation keys: **every other page**
Method for accent marks: **after syllable**
Order of definitions: **frequency of use**
Illustrative examples: **yes**
Illustrative quotations: **no**
Placement of etymologies: **before definitions**
Synonym studies: **yes**
Word history studies: **yes**
Usage studies: **yes**
Pictorial illustrations (number): **400**
Encyclopedic information: **in separate sections**
Special features:
- **Vocabulary excludes obscene and offensive words**
- **Writing style guide**
- **Foreign words and phrases**
- **Charts of signs and symbols, scientific measures, metric conversions**

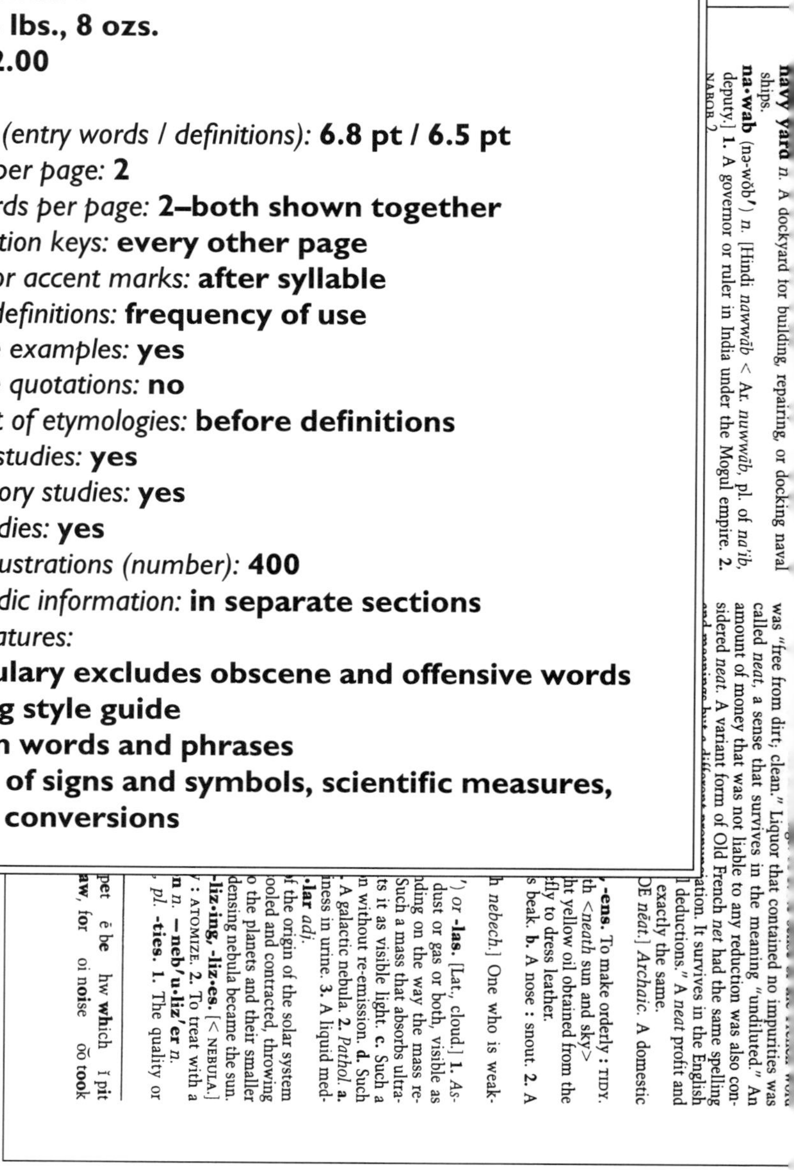

navy yard *n.* A dockyard for building, repairing, or docking naval ships.
na•wab (nə-wŏb′) *n.* [Hindi *nawwāb* < Ar. *nuwwāb*, pl. of *na'ib*, deputy.] **1.** A governor or ruler in India under the Mogul empire. **2.** NABOB 2.

was "free from dirt; clean." Liquor that contained no impurities was called *neat*, a sense that survives in the meaning "undiluted." An amount of money that was not liable to any reduction was also considered *neat*. A variant form of Old French *net* had the same spelling ... ation. It survives in the English ... deductions." A *neat* profit and ... exactly the same.
... OE *nēat*.] *Archaic.* A domestic
-ens. To make orderly : TIDY.
th <*neath* sun and sky>
ht yellow oil obtained from the
fly to dress leather.
s beak. **b.** A nose : snout. **2.** A
h *nebech*.] One who is weak-
′) *or* **-las.** [Lat., cloud.] **1.** *As-*
dust or gas or both, visible as
nding on the way the mass re-
Such a mass that absorbs ultra-
ts it as visible light. **c.** Such a
n without re-emission. **d.** Such
. A galactic nebula. **2.** *Pathol.* **a.**
ness in urine. **3.** A liquid med-
-lar *adj.*
f the origin of the solar system
ooled and contracted, throwing
o the planets and their smaller
densing nebula became the sun.
-liz•ing, -liz•es. [< NEBULA.]
; ATOMIZE. **2.** To treat with a
n *n.* **—neb′u•liz′er** *n.*
, *pl.* **-ties. 1.** The quality or

pet ē **be** hw **which** ĭ pit
aw, **for** oi **noise** ŏŏ **took**

na•vic•u•lar (nə-vĭk′yə-lər) *n.* [LLat. *navicularis* < Lat. *navicula,* dim. of *navis,* ship.] **1.** A bone of the wrist shaped like a comma. **2.** The concave bone in front of the anklebone on the instep of the foot. —*adj.* Shaped like a boat.

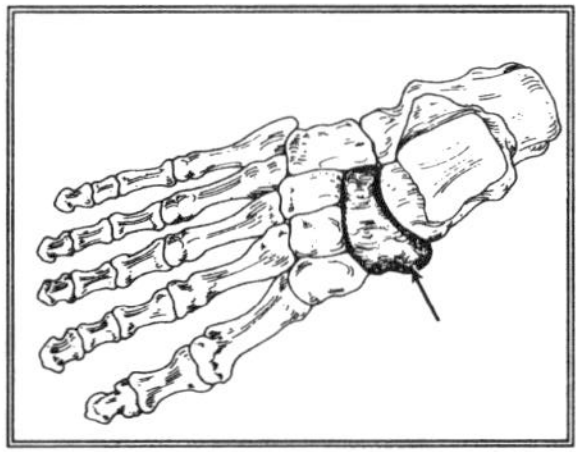

navicular

nav•i•ga•ble (năv′ĭ-gə-bəl) *adj.* **1.** Wide or deep enough for vehicular passage. **2.** Capable of being steered. —Used of vessels or aircraft. **—nav′i•ga•bil′i•ty** *n.* **—nav′i•ga•bly** *adv.*

nav•i•gate (năv′ĭ-gāt′) *v.* **-gat•ed, -gat•ing, -gates.** [Lat. *navigare, navigat-* : *navis,* ship + *agere,* to direct.] —*vt.* **1.** To record, plan, and control the position and course of (a ship or aircraft). **2.** To follow a planned course on, across, or through <*navigate* a river> —*vi.* **1.** To control the course of a ship or aircraft. **2.** To voyage over water in a boat or ship : SAIL. **3.** *Informal.* **a.** To make one's way. **b.** To walk <too drunk to *navigate*>

nav•i•ga•tion (năv′ĭ-gā′shən) *n.* **1.** The theory and practice of navigating, esp. the charting of a course for a ship or aircraft. **2.** Travel or traffic by vessels, esp. commercial shipping. **—nav′i•ga′tion•al** *adj.*

nav•i•ga•tor (năv′ĭ-gā′tər) *n.* **1.** One who navigates. **2.** A device that directs the course of an aircraft or missile.

nav•vy (năv′ē) *n., pl.* **-vies.** [Alteration of NAVIGATOR, canal laborer (obs.).] *Chiefly Brit.* A laborer, esp. one employed in construction or excavation projects.

na•vy (nā′vē) *n., pl.* **-vies.** [ME *navie* < OFr. < VLat. *navia < Lat. *navis,* ship.] **1.** All of a nation's warships. **2.** *often* **Navy.** A nation's entire military organization for sea warfare and defense. **3.** A group of ships : FLEET. **4.** Navy blue.

navy bean *n.* [From its former use as a standard provision of the U.S. Navy.] One of several varieties of the kidney bean, cultivated for their nutritious white seeds.

West Germany.] An extinct species or race of humans, *Homo neanderthalensis,* living during the late Pleistocene epoch in the Old World and associated with Middle Paleolithic tools.

ne•an•throp•ic (nē′ən-thrŏp′ĭk) *adj.* [NE(O)- + ANTHROP(O)- + -IC.] Of or relating to members of the extant species *Homo sapiens* as compared with other, now extinct species of *Homo.*

Ne•a•pol•i•tan (nē′ə-pŏl′ĭ-tən) *adj.* Of, belonging to, or characteristic of Naples, Italy. —*n.* A resident or native of Naples, Italy.

Neapolitan ice cream *n.* Brick ice cream with layers of different colors and flavors.

neap tide (nēp) *n.* [ME *neep < OE *nēp(flōd),* neap (tide).] A tide of lowest range, occurring when the sun and moon are in quadrature.

near (nîr) *adv.* **-er, -est.** [ME *ner* < OE *nēar,* comp. adv. of *nēah,* near.] **1.** To, at, or within a short distance or interval in space or time. **2.** Nearly : almost <*near* played out> **3.** With or in a close relationship. —*adj.* **-er, -est. 1.** Close in time, position, space, or degree <the *near* past> **2.** Closely related by kinship or association : INTIMATE. **3.** Failing or succeeding by a very small margin <a *near* bull's-eye> **4.** Closely corresponding to or resembling an original <a *near* copy> **5. a.** Closer of two or more. **b.** On the left side of a vehicle or draft team. **6.** Short and direct <the *nearest* route to the airport> **7.** Stingy : cheap. —*prep.* Close to <a motel *near* town> —*v.* **neared, near•ing, nears.** —*vt.* To come close or closer to. —*vi.* To draw near or nearer : APPROACH. **—near′ness** *n.*

★ ***syns:*** NEAR, CLOSE, IMMEDIATE, NEARBY, NIGH *adj. core meaning* : not far from another in space, time, or relation <The airport was *near* the town.> <They were *near* to me in age.>

near beer *n.* A malt liquor not containing enough alcohol to be considered an alcoholic beverage.

near•by (nîr′bī′) *adj.* & *adv.* Close at hand.

Ne•arc•tic (nē-ärk′tĭk, -är′tĭk) *adj.* [NE(O)- + ARCTIC.] Of or designating the zoogeographic region that includes the Arctic and Temperate areas of North America and Greenland.

near•ly (nîr′lē) *adv.* **1.** Almost but not quite. **2.** Closely : intimately <were *nearly* associated for years>

near•sight•ed (nîr′sī′tĭd) *adj.* Not able to see distant objects clearly : MYOPIC. **—near′sight′ed•ly** *adv.* **—near′sight′ed•ness** *n.*

neat[1] (nēt) *adj.* **-er, -est.** [OFr. *net* < Lat. *nitidus,* elegant < *nitēre,* to shine.] **1.** Clean and orderly : TIDY. **2.** Orderly and exact in procedure : SYSTEMATIC. **3.** Characterized by creativity and skill : ADROIT. **4.** Not diluted or mixed with other substances <*neat* liqueur> **5.** NET[2] 1. **6.** *Slang.* Wonderful : terrific <went to a *neat* picnic> —*adv.* Without dilution : STRAIGHT <takes whiskey *neat*> **—neat′ly** *adv.* **—neat′ness** *n.*

Title: **The World Book Dictionary**
Publisher: **World Book Publishing**
Most recent copyright: **2000**
No. of volumes: **2**
Weight: **5 lbs. (each volume)**
Price: **$89.00**
Type size (entry words / definitions): **7 pt / 7 pt**
Columns per page: **3**
Guide words per page: **1**
Pronunciation keys: **every other page**
Method for accent marks: **after syllable**
Order of definitions: **frequency of use**
Illustrative examples: **yes**
Illustrative quotations: **yes**
Placement of etymologies: **after definitions**
Synonym studies: **yes**
Word history studies: **no**
Usage studies: **yes**
Pictorial illustrations (number): **3,000**
Encyclopedic information: **not included**
Special features:

- **Vocabulary excludes obscene and offensive words**
- **Vocabulary includes many foreign words and phrases**
- **Grammar, spelling, punctuation, and writing guides**
- **Lists of vocabulary words for third grade through college**
- **Guides to pronouncing foreign languages**
- **Charts of signs and symbols, weights and measures, proofreaders' marks**

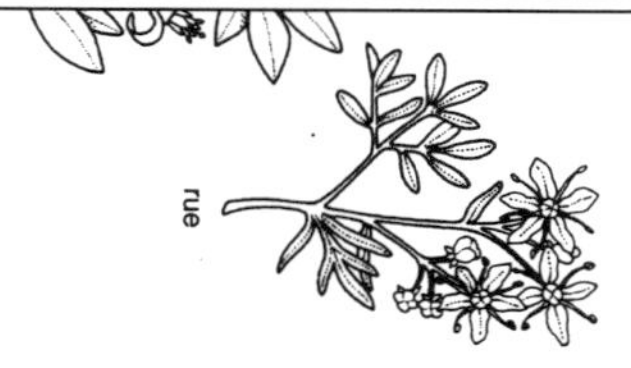

ru|bric|i|ty (rü bris′ə tē), *n.* **1** the assumption of a red color: *the periodical ... rubricity of the Nile* (Auckland C. Geddes). **2** adherence to liturgical rubrics.
ru|bus (rü′bəs), *n., pl.* **-bus**. any bramble, such as the blackberry, raspberry, and dewberry. [< New Latin *Rubus* the genus name < Latin *rubus* blackberry, bramble]
ru|by (rü′bē), *n., pl.* **-bies**, *adj.* — ***n.*** **1** a clear, hard, red precious stone. It is a variety of corundum. Real rubies are very rare. *Formula:* Al_2O_3 **2** its color, a deep, glowing red: *the natural ruby of your cheek* (Shakespeare). **3** something made of ruby, especially a bearing in a watch. **4** red wine: *Still the Vine her ancient Ruby yields* (Edward FitzGerald). **5** *British.* a size of printing type; approximately 5½ points. In the United States it is called *agate.* **6** *British Slang.* blood.
— ***adj.*** deep, glowing red: *ruby lips, ruby wine.*
[< Old French *rubis,* plural of *rubi,* ultimately < Latin *rubeus* red] — **ru′by|like′**, *adj.*
Ru|by (rü′bē), *n., pl.* **-bies**. a red-fleshed variety of grapefruit developed from natural sports of other varieties.
ru|by-crowned kinglet (rü′bē kround′), a tiny, grayish, North American bird, the male of which has a bright ruby patch on the crown.
ruby silver, **1** = pyrargyrite. **2** = proustite.
ruby spaniel, a chestnut red variety of the English toy spaniel.
ruby spinel, = spinel ruby.
ru|by|tail (rü′bē tāl′), *n.* any one of various small, solitary, stinging insects that are brilliantly colored and lay their eggs in the nests of other insects. One variety has a ruby-colored abdomen.
ru|by|throat (rü′bē thrōt′), *n.* = ruby-throated hummingbird.
ru|by-throat|ed hummingbird (rü′bē thrō′tid), a hummingbird of eastern North America with bright-green plumage above. The male also has a brilliant-red throat.
R.U.C., Royal Ulster Constabulary.
ru|cer|vine (rü sėr′vīn, -vin), *adj.* of or having to do with a group of large East Indian deer that have branching antlers and long tines extending forward over the brow. [< New Latin *Rucervus* the genus name (< Malay *rūsa* deer + Latin *cervus* deer) + English *-ine*[1]]

rudd (rud), *n.* a red-finned, European freshwater fish related to the carp. [earlier *rowde,* apparently a use of *rud* redness, Old English *rudu;* see etym. under **rud**]
***rud|der** (rud′ər), *n.* **1** a movable flat piece of wood or metal at the rear end of a boat or ship, by which it is steered. **2** a similar piece on an aircraft (for right-and-left steering). **3** *Figurative.* a person or thing that guides, directs, or controls. [Middle English *roder* < Old English *rōthor*]

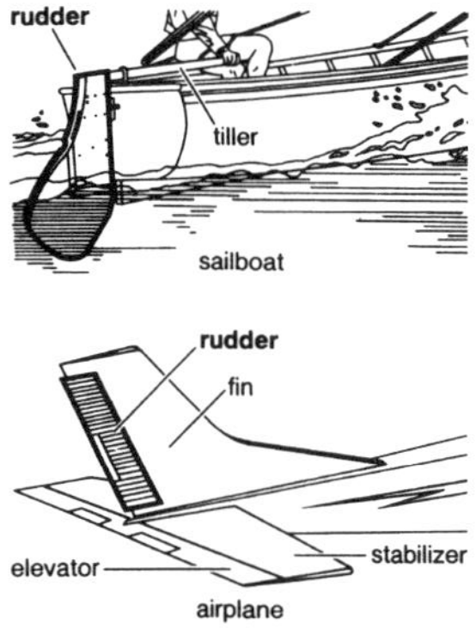

***rudder**
definitions 1, 2

rudder bar, a foot-operated bar in the cockpit of certain light airplanes, to which the control cables leading to the rudder are attached.
rud|dered (rud′ərd), *adj.* having a rudder.
rud|der|head (rud′ər hed′), *n.* the upper end of the rudder, into which the tiller is fitted.
rud|der|less (rud′ər lis), *adj.* without a rudder or controls: *a rudderless boat.* (*Figurative.*) *Left rudderless, Pakistan drifted on the currents of opportunism, intrigue and corruption* (Atlantic). SYN: drfiting, aimless.
rud|der|post (rud′ər pōst′), *n.* **1** an extension of the sternpost on which the rudder is hung. **2** = rudderstock.
rud|der|stock (rud′ər stok′), *n.* the part of a rudder by which it is connected to the ship.
rud|dle (rud′əl), *n., v.,* **-dled, -dling**. — ***n.*** = red ocher.

Gray). SYN: primitive. **6** belonging to the poor or to uncultured people; without luxury or elegance; simple: *a rude, primitive culture. The temple ... is of rude design and indifferent execution* (Amelia B. Edwards). **7** not fully or properly developed. **8** robust; sturdy; vigorous: *rude health, rude strength.* **9** *Archaic.* inexpert; unskilled. [< Latin *rudis*] — **rude′ly**, *adv.* — **rude′ness**, *n.*
ru|der|al (rü′dər əl), *adj., n.* — ***adj.*** growing in rubbish or waste places: *a ruderal plant, ruderal vegetation.*
— ***n.*** a ruderal weed: ... *ruderals of open ground* (New Scientist).
[< New Latin *ruderalis* < Latin *rūdera* (plural of *rūdus* broken stone) + *-ālis* al[1]]
rudes|by (rüdz′bē), *n., pl.* **-bies**. *Archaic.* a rude or unmannerly fellow: *Rudesby, be gone!* (Shakespeare). [< *rude* + *sby,* an ending of proper names, such as *Crosby, Hornsby*]
Rü|des|heim|er (rʏ′dəs hī′mər), *n.* a fine white Rhine wine. [< German *Rüdesheimer* < *Rüdesheim,* a town on the Rhine]
ru|di|ment (rü′də mənt), *n.* **1** a part to be learned first; beginning: *the rudiments of arithmetic.* [*He*] *received the first rudiments of his education at a little free-school* (Richard Graves). **2** something in an early stage; undeveloped or imperfect form: *a youth ... who apparently had not in him even the rudiments of worldly successfulness* (Arnold Bennett). **3** an organ or part incompletely developed in size or structure: *the rudiments of wings on a baby chick.* [< Latin *rudīmentum* < *rudis* rude, ignorant]
ru|di|men|tal (rü′də men′təl), *adj.* = rudimentary.
ru|di|men|ta|ry (rü′də men′tər ē, -trē), *adj.* **1** that is to be learned or studied first; elementary: *It is almost impossible to learn multiplication without knowing the rudimentary steps of addition.* SYN: See syn. under **elementary**. **2** in an early stage of development; undeveloped: *rudimentary wings.* SYN: embryonic. — **ru′di|men′ta|ri|ly**, *adv.* — **ru′di|men′ta|ri|ness**, *n.*
rue[1] (rü), *v.,* **rued**, **ru|ing**, *n.* — ***v.t.*** to be sorry for; regret; repent: *She will rue the day she insulted your mother. Thou shalt rue this treason* (Shakespeare). *Was ever son so rued a father's death?* (Shakespeare). SYN: deplore.
— ***v.i.*** *Archaic.* to feel sorrow; lament.
— ***n.*** sorrow; regret; repentance: *With rue my heart is laden For golden friends I had* (A. E.

Decide which of these preferences are important to you in selecting your "family dictionary." Mark those preferences in the first column with an X. From the information and sample pages shown on pp. 46–69, rate each dictionary (+ or –) on these important preferences.	**Important Preferences**	***The American Heritage College Dictionary, Third Edition***	***The American Heritage Dictionary of the English Language, Third Edition***
Is the copyright date recent enough to ensure an up-to-date vocabulary? *(see page 26)*			
Do you prefer a dictionary that is published as a single volume?			
Is the weight light enough to afford easy handling? *(see page 23)*			
Is the price of the dictionary within your budget?			
Is the type size of the entry words and the definitions large enough for easy reading? *(see page 28)*			
Do you prefer that your dictionary have 2 columns per page or 3?			
How should guide words be displayed: 1 per page? 2 together? 2 left and right? *(see page 29)*			
Do you prefer to have a pronunciations key visible from every page? *(see page 30)*			
Which method do you prefer for the placement of accent marks? *(see page 31)*			
Do you prefer definitions arranged in historical order or according to frequency? *(see page 32)*			
Do you want your dictionary to include illustrative examples in its definitions? *(see page 34)*			
Do you prefer etymologies placed before or after the definitions? *(see page 35)*			
Do you prefer a dictionary that includes paragraph-length synonym studies? *(see page 37)*			
Do you prefer a dictionary that includes paragraph-length word history studies? *(see page 37)*			
Do you prefer a dictionary that includes paragraph-length usage studies? *(see page 39)*			
Do you prefer a dictionary that has pictorial illustrations? How many are enough? *(see page 40)*			
Should encyclopedic information appear in the main body or in separate sections? *(see page 40)*			
Which dictionaries include special features that are particularly useful to you? *(see page 41)*			

The Concise Oxford Dictionary, Tenth Edition	*The DK Illustrated Oxford Dictionary*	*Encarta World English Dictionary*	*Merriam-Webster's Collegiate® Dictionary, Tenth Edition*	*The Oxford American Dictionary and Language Guide*	*Random House Webster's College Dictionary*	*Webster's American Family Dictionary*	*Webster's New World College Dictionary, Fourth Edition*	*Webster's II New College Dictionary*	*The World Book Dictionary*

USING A DICTIONARY

"One point is clear, however:
whether we are parents or teachers or . . .
role models of whatever sort . . .
only example, not precept,
will prevail."

Kenneth G. Wilson
in *Van Winkle's Return*

In the quotation above, Professor Kenneth G. Wilson was describing why we shouldn't simply expect our children, our students, or our employees to adopt a level of English that we don't use ourselves. The adage "practice what you preach" holds true because the practice itself—the modeling, the constant demonstration of what is expected—is the most effective form of preaching you can do.

Indeed, one of the fundamental beliefs of Family Learning is that this principle applies not just to language education, but to every area of study—math, geography, even character development.

"Only example, not precept, will prevail." If we want our children to develop a mastery of English that will allow them to speak and write with both precision and grace, we must show them *by our example* that acquiring such skill is an unexceptional part of our daily self-improvement and that our dictionary plays a central role in our own learning. The most powerful technique there is to help children acquire a "dictionary habit" is simply wondering aloud—in the presence of your children—about a certain usage, and then reaching for a dictionary—in the presence of your children—to satisfy your curiosity. Having children watch you use your "family dictionary," and encouraging them to use it as well, says to them that you care about the way language is used and can be used, and that you want them to care about these things, too.

So, not only do we want to start using the dictionary more frequently for our own knowledge and improvement, we also want to "get caught" using the dictionary in front of our children. Perhaps it's a word or phrase during a dinner table conversation that sparks an inquiry such as "I wonder where that word came from?"; perhaps it's a curious pronunciation used by a television newscaster or by a character in a show or a movie that your family is watching. These are "teachable moments," so don't hesitate to take advantage of them right away. Take the dictionary to the dinner table or to the sofa and satisfy your curiosity while

Investigating words from television

you demonstrate an important learning behavior to your children. Soon you'll be asking them to locate the word in question and read its definition, pronunciation, or origin. Later, you may not have to ask at all, for they might—just might—come to see this activity as a pleasurable one that secures their place and membership in the family.

Have children locate words in dictionary

Breaking the Code

The great teacher and philosopher Mortimer J. Adler, who wrote more than a hundred books including a classic titled *How to Read a Book*, believed that "One of the first rules as to how to read a book is to know what sort of book it is. That means knowing what the author's intention was and what sort of thing you can expect to find in his work." This principle holds just as true for dictionaries as for novels and biographies. You need to understand clearly the intentions and the purposes that your dictionary was designed to meet. What did the people who compiled your dictionary want it to be, and how did they design it to achieve that end? For example, did they design your dictionary to report how words *are* spelled and pronounced, or how they *should be* spelled and pronounced? Did they choose to list definitions according to their historical order or according to their frequency of use?

Questions like these must be cleared up early on, or else you might assume your dictionary is telling you one thing when it is actually saying something quite different.

Fortunately, all these matters can be put to rest rather quickly because every dictionary includes a section in its first several pages—before you get to the entry words beginning with *A*—that lays out the exact plan and design for every feature of the book. This section is usually titled "Guide to the Dictionary," "Using This Dictionary," or simply "Explanatory Notes," and it is always broken down into categories and sub-categories that will lead you to the specific understandings that you are seeking.

What is your dictionary *really* saying when it lists two or more different spellings for the same word? You can find out by reading the section labeled "Variants" in the guide at the front of the book. Where does your dictionary tell you to place the hyphen when you find it necessary to break a certain word at the end of a line? Just look under the section labeled "Syllables" or "Word Division."

sections labeled "Variants" & "Syllables"

Yet, the process of understanding a dictionary before you read it is different from understanding most other books in that the way dictionaries pack so much information into a relatively small space is by using a great variety of symbols and abbreviations. You have to know what the pronunciation and stress symbols mean, for example, before you can understand the exact sound that your dictionary is trying to describe. Here, again, the guide pages in the front of the book tell you everything you need to know, usually under the heading "Pronunciation."

sections labeled "Pronunciation" & "Etymology"

The various symbols that condense the entire history of a word into a mere line or two can also be deciphered with the explanations that are found under the heading "Etymology" or "Word Origins." Almost all dictionaries, for example, use the < symbol to mean "derived from" or "taken from," and they use abbreviations to identify languages and periods other than modern English (*OF* = Old French, *Gk.* = Greek, *ME* = Middle English). If a key to these abbreviations does not appear in the guide pages, look for it in the listing of "Contents," which follows the title and copyright page.

The "Guide to the Dictionary" will also tell you the precise meaning that your dictionary applies to the usage labels it has assigned to guide your choice and use of words. But if you don't understand what your dictionary is telling you by labeling a word "non-standard" or "colloquial," how can such advice serve as much of a guide?

Back to Basics

Most dictionaries assume that you already have a basic understanding of the parts of speech, and so they label each entry word according to the way it can be used in a sentence (*noun*, *verb*, *adjective*, and so on). This presents little difficulty for most people—with one glaring exception: What are "transitive" and "intransitive" verbs?

When your dictionary labels a verb as "transitive" (abbreviated *vt.* or *tr.v.*), it merely shows that, when used in this way, the action of the verb passes from the subject to someone or something that acts as the direct object.

The entire family signed the dictionary.

In this case, the verb *signed* is a transitive verb because it has a direct object (*dictionary*), which receives the action of the verb. The easiest way to find the direct object is to ask Who? or What? after the subject and the verb:

Family signed *what?* (answer: *dictionary*)

Intransitive verbs have no direct object.

My dog always barks when I come home.

The questions "My dog barks *who?*" or "My dog barks *what*" are meaningless because there is no direct object to complete the action of the verb. So, in this sentence, the verb *barks* is an intransitive verb.

- *bark*
- *sleep*
- *look*
- *laugh*
- *sit*
- *set*
- *lie*
- *lay*

Bark is one of those verbs (others include *sleep*, *look*, and *laugh*) that seem to have only intransitive uses; that is, you probably can't think of a sentence in which these verbs could possibly have a direct object. But your dictionary will list both intransitive and transitive examples for each. Check them out.

This distinction between transitive and intransitive verbs is essential in understanding the proper uses of the verbs *sit* and *set*, *lie* and *lay*.

Inflected Forms

Another assumption that dictionaries make about your knowledge of English grammar and usage is that you understand how nouns, verbs, adjectives, and adverbs change their spellings to fit their use in different sentences. Most dictionaries, therefore, don't even show the plural form of nouns when the change from the singular is made in the "regular" way (that is, adding *-s* or *-es*), nor do they show the comparative and superlative forms of adjectives that are formed in the "regular" way (that is, adding *-er* and *-est*). However, when these "inflected forms" are created in irregular ways, or when there might be some reason for confusion about their spelling (Should I double the final consonant?), the dictionary will either spell out the complete form or show the suffix that must be added to the entry word.

la·zy /láyzee/ (**-zi·er, -zi·est**) *adj.* **1. NOT WANTING TO WORK** unwilling to do any work or make an effort **2. CONDUCIVE TO IDLENESS** contributing to an unwillingness to work or make an effort ○ *a lazy spring day* **3. SLOW** moving slowly ○ *a lazy river* **4.** AGRIC **UPSIDE DOWN** shown as a brand on livestock as a letter or number rotated 90 degrees from an upright position ○ *a lazy H* [Mid-16thC. Origin uncertain: perhaps from Low German *lasich* "feeble, tired."] —**la·zi·ly** *adv.* —**la·zi·ness** *n.*

from *Webster's II New College Dictionary*

You can learn precisely how your dictionary treats these inflected forms, including the method it uses to list the principal parts of verbs (past tense, past participle, present participle), by looking under the heading "Inflected Forms" in the guide pages at the front of the dictionary.

sections labeled "Inflected Forms"

Talking about Words

One of the ways that children benefit from participating in dictionary investigations with their parents is that they acquire an understanding of the words that are commonly used to talk about words. When they hear their parents (and their brothers or sisters) use words like *singular, plural, syllable, synonym, antonym, prefix, suffix, long e,* and *Latin* in casual conversations that result from, or in, a trip to the dictionary, children are better prepared to understand language lessons they will receive in a classroom. These terms will not seem like a foreign language to them, or a special vocabulary that is used only in school.

Use "school" words at home

So, don't be afraid to talk about the parts of speech, and to let your dictionary provide examples of how the same word can be used in several ways, each a different part of speech. (One of my favorite examples is the word *round:* adjective, noun, verb—both transitive and intransitive—adverb, and preposition.) Let your children hear you use the word *etymology* when you talk about word origins, and *boldface* or *italic* when you identify the typefaces of entry words and usage labels.

Use "round" in six different ways

Use specialized vocabulary to discuss words

Even a Dictionary Has Its Limits

I have said that a good "family dictionary" is the most valuable self-help aid you can own for the study and improvement of language in your home. But you must keep in mind that a dictionary is not designed to show you *how* to improve your spelling, your vocabulary, your pronunciation, or your choice of words. A dictionary provides the *what* in our quest for language improvement—the words, spellings, pronunciations, and meanings that make up the language called Modern English. A dictionary does not separate interesting words from uninteresting ones, nor does it highlight useful new words that you might want to add to your vocabulary. There are, however, many other books that are designed to function precisely in these ways and are available at your local public library.

Word Choice.

Browse the 808 and 420–428 sections of your library's adult collection and you'll find many guidebooks to help you improve your choice and use of words. These books help you focus on specific usage problems that you can then investigate in your dictionary and mark for your family's attention. For example, do you know why the use of the word *literally* in the following sentence is considered to be an improper or nonstandard usage?

• *literally*

> The players were literally frozen stiff
> by the end of the game.

Books like *Woe Is I*, by Patricia T. O'Conner [428.2 OCO], and *The Elements of Style*, a classic by William Strunk and E. B. White [808 STR], will work in conjunction with your dictionary to tell you not only what *is* in the realm of word usage, but also what *should be*. Then you can make a more informed decision yourself, and you can choose to use or not use certain words or meanings based on your knowledge, not simply on what you are accustomed to hearing.

Vocabulary.

Among these library resources you'll find books that help you develop a larger and more precise vocabulary, too. *When Is a Pig a Hog?* by Bernice Randall [422.03 RAN], is one of several guides to distinguishing between the distinct and separate meanings of seemingly similar words. *Dos, Don'ts & Maybes of English Usage*, by Theodore M. Bernstein [428 BER], and *The Appropriate Word*, by J. N. Hook [428 HOO], also focus on pairs of words that have precise meanings and uses, but are frequently confused and misused. (Did you know that *disinterested* and *uninterested* have two quite different meanings? Let your dictionary teach you which is which.)

- ***disinterested***
- ***uninterested***

Pronunciations.

Precise pronunciations are another matter for which you will need additional resources to work in conjunction with your dictionary. Because dictionaries have adopted a "descriptive" rather than a "prescriptive" approach to pronunciations, all you will know (in most cases) from the variants that are listed for a certain entry word is the comparative frequency of their use.

The problem here is that people often make judgments about others based solely upon the way they hear them pronounce certain words. Whether people *should* make these judgments or not is irrelevant; the fact is that your pronunciations *will* characterize you in the minds of some people, and you won't know who these people are.

But because you can choose to use one pronunciation instead of another, you have the power to create a favorable impression instead of an unfavorable one, at least among those people who are impressionable about such matters. By pronouncing a word one way, you may appear to be rather uneducated or imprecise or uncaring about the language you use. But the alternative pronunciation may—all by itself—create an entirely different, and positive, impression about you.

Your dictionary will not, and cannot, tell you the impressions that each variant pronunciation will have upon your listeners. But there are resources in the 421–423 sections of your library's general collection (and reference collection) that will explain to you what other people may be thinking when they hear you pronounce a word in a certain way, and why your choice of that particular pronunciation might lead them to make that particular judgment.

Among my favorite resources for this purpose are three books by Charles Harrington Elster: *There Is No Zoo in Zoology, Is There a Cow in Moscow?*, and *The Big Book of Beastly Mispronunciations*. Here you will find guidance for developing your own personal pronunciation standards, so that when your dictionary tells you that words like *assuage, athlete, heinous, machination, nuclear, plethora,* and *zoology* can be pronounced, and are pronounced, in more than one way, you can choose the pronunciation that conveys to others precisely what you want to say about yourself.

- *assuage*
- *athlete*
- *heinous*
- *machination*
- *nuclear*
- *plethora*
- *zoology*

Word Histories.

There is another set of resource books in your local public library that will encourage you to read your dictionary and will provide interesting stories to tell your children. These books are collections of amusing and entertaining word histories—the sometimes fascinating stories about how and why the words we use today came to be the words we use today. Books like *Thereby Hangs a Tale* and *Heavens to Betsy!,* by Charles Earle Funk [422 FUN], and *Word Mysteries & Histories*, by the Editors of The American Heritage Dictionaries [422.03 WOR], can provide the memorable hooks that help us understand that words are not simply created out of thin air (*zoot* and *googol* are the only exceptions that come to mind). Each of our words has a traceable history that tells us the reason for its being in the form it is today. (Did you know that the words *tawdry* and *maudlin* are really alterations of the names Saint Audrey and Mary Magdalene?)

- *tawdry*
- *maudlin*

"But It's in the Dictionary!"

Dictionaries include words of all kinds—hundreds of thousands of them. Some of these words you know already, and some will become useful additions to your vocabulary. But the fact is that you will never hear, or read, or have occasion to use the vast majority of all the entry words in the book. Oh, you *could* use a word like *arachibutyrophobia* someday, I suppose, if you happened to find yourself discussing some people's fear of having peanut butter stick to the roof of their mouth (that's what it means). But even if you know this word, you wouldn't just bring it up in casual conversation because it would be completely inappropriate in practically any imaginable setting or group. And you *could* choose to say or write the word *irregardless*, too, but because it is almost always used by people who don't know or don't care that the word *regardless* already exists, it almost always brands the user as being either ignorant or careless about language, and so might be appropriate only among people who either don't know or don't care what you are saying.

Learning the appropriateness of words is just as important—perhaps more so—than learning the words themselves. Just as a baseball cap *can* be worn, and *can* be worn backwards as well, this would not be appropriate attire if you were interviewing for a job and wanted to make a good impression.

So, too, there are words that are used every day in casual street speech that are completely inappropriate in polite conversations, business communications, or in settings that include people you respect and admire. The child who is reprimanded for using an obscene word or phrase during a dinner table discussion, and whose retort is "But it's in the dictionary!" needs to learn a vitally important lesson about dictionaries (as well as a lesson about appropriate language).

Words get into a dictionary because they *have been used*, not because they *should be used*.

Vulgar, obscene words *do* exist; they *are* words, and so they are in the dictionary. But just because a word exists (or a baseball cap, for that matter) does not mean that it is appropriate in every situation. Words get into a dictionary because they *have been used*, not because they *should be used*. Think about it this way: With every new edition of a dictionary, certain entry words are also taken *out*, not because they can't be used any longer, but because they aren't being used any longer.

We can't expect dictionary editors to purge their books of every single word that might be considered offensive, in part because there are many good and respectable words that have offensive or vulgar meanings and uses. (Three of the "family dictionaries" shown in this book, however, have made a conscious effort to delete obscenities from their entry words and definitions wherever possible: *Webster's American Family Dictionary*, published by Random House; *Webster's II New College Dictionary*, published by Houghton Mifflin; and *The World Book Dictionary*.) What we can expect is that our "family dictionary" will act as a guidebook in helping us and our children understand what certain words say about us when we use them.

We can expect our dictionary to warn us with usage labels, such as *obscene* or *vulgar*, that if we choose to employ these words or usages in our speech or writing, it is we who will be considered obscene or vulgar. A label like *offensive* tells us not only that this word or phrase is considered insulting and derogatory by some people or groups, but that in using this word or phrase, we will be considered offensive.

Sure, "it's in the dictionary," and so are *irregardless* and *arachibutyrophobia*, too. But you choose not to use these words because the first makes you appear ignorant, and you can't think of any appropriate use for the second. Maybe you'll come to these same judgments about using obscenities, vulgarities, and racial or ethnic slurs, as well. That's the point: It's all up to you.

Russell's Rules for Using a Family Dictionary

Once you start to appreciate the decisions that have been made in constructing your dictionary, and once you start to become familiar with the design and the arrangement of the dictionary that you have in your home, you can then start to take advantage of it—to put it through its paces and draw out of it the worlds of information that lie waiting to be tapped by anyone interested enough and knowledgeable enough to unleash its vast learning potential.

The "family dictionary" is an indispensable part of the practice I call Family Learning.

But just how do you begin to mine this most valuable learning resource? Not cover-to-cover, that's for sure. And not alone, either, for just as in every other area of learning, the combined power and encouragement of the family—no matter how large or small that family might be—provides both the opportunities to learn from the dictionary and the applications for that learning, as well. The "family dictionary" is an indispensable part of the practice I call Family Learning, and those families who appreciate and enjoy learning together seem always to revere their dictionary as a valued part of their home.

So, here are a few suggestions—yes, I think *suggestions* is better than *rules*—that I have found to be extremely helpful in getting adults and children to feel comfortable and confident in using their dictionary as a learning tool. It should be noted, though, that all of these suggestions assume that you have already become familiar with your dictionary, and you have read the introductory sections titled “How to Use This Dictionary” or “Guide to the Dictionary,” as I have recommended earlier in this book.

#1 *Remove the paper dust jacket from your dictionary.*

Dictionaries have to be used in order for them to do anyone any good, and in the process of being used, they will be handled and handed back and forth. This is why the best “family dictionaries” are not the bigger-than-a-breadbox, unabridged versions you usually see on a pedestal or a table stand. These mammoth volumes may be masterpieces of lexicography and scholarship, but they are heavy to lift and hold, and almost impossible to pass around. A good “family dictionary,” instead, should invite people to use it—children and adults alike—by being of a size and weight that allows everyone to handle it comfortably and repeatedly.

I was quite surprised to find that the paper dust jacket that always comes with a new “collegiate” dictionary also discourages the handling and use of the book. Really, it's true. People tend to worry that this paper cover might get nicked or "dog-eared" or marred in some way, and the more it happens—a little nick here, a stain or smudge there, and so on—the less the dictionary gets used, or passed around. And woe to the one who creates a noticeable tear in this beautiful, but absolutely useless, tribute to Madison Avenue.

If you want to ensure that your dictionary is handled with care in your home, you must first make sure that it is handled at all. The more everyone in your home uses the book and sees it as a valuable part of your family life, the more likely it is that they will treat it with thoughtfulness and respect. (See #3)

#2 *Keep the dictionary within easy reach.*

Where is your dictionary? Upstairs on a bookshelf, or in a desk drawer, or maybe in the basement? If your home is like most homes, your dictionary will not be immediately accessible, and so when you hear a strange word on television or when you question a particular usage in the newspaper, you don't dash upstairs or down, and hunt for your dictionary so that you can hunt for the word in question. Not if you're like most people, because the rest of us just sit there telling ourselves that we'll remember that curious word or phrase and look it up later, when we happen to be in the room that has the dictionary and when it happens to be within arm's reach. But how many times have you promised this to yourself only to have the word that initiated the search vanish without a trace from your memory by the time any dictionary came into view?

It is very normal and very natural to forget the words that stimulated your curiosity after just a few minutes, or to forget why you were curious about them in the first place. While natural and understandable, it is still disappointing because you had created a special moment—an instant when your curiosity and your learning interests were aroused by something you saw or heard in the real world, and you threw that opportunity away simply because the resource that would have answered your questions was not close enough at hand.

Where is language used most often in your home?

Well, you could solve the problem by placing a dictionary in every room in your house, and, indeed, there are families who make a point to peruse book sales and garage sales for inexpensive, used dictionaries to place in various rooms. But most families, if they have a dictionary at all, have just one good dictionary at their disposal. So the solution usually lies in making that dictionary more available and more convenient for answering whatever language questions might be generated from newspapers, television, and family conversations.

Where is language used most often in your home? If you consider all the types of reading and listening and talking that involve language use, then I'll bet that the living room or family room comes out on top. Here is where people read magazines and watch television and listen to the radio and CD's. Here, then, is where those curious words and spellings and usages are most likely to arise, and so here is where your "family dictionary" should have its home. If you read the paper in the same chair every night, place the dictionary somewhere within arm's reach of that chair. If you watch television together as a family, place your dictionary on a coffee table or in a central and convenient location so that it can be referred to inconspicuously by anyone who hears a curious word or phrase and wonders about its meaning, or its use, or its origin. This not only allows you immediate access to this most valuable learning resource, but it also guarantees that your children will see you reaching for the dictionary, and that they will come to accept this act as a common and customary response to any language stimulus that any family member might receive from a news broadcast, a movie, or even a situation comedy.

It is also a good idea to keep a pencil nearby and a sheet or two of notepaper inside the dictionary. When you investigate a word and learn something new (its spelling, meaning, pronunciation, etc.), jot that word down so that you have an ongoing list of words you have already researched. Glancing over

Keep a word list in your dictionary

this list after each new investigation will reinforce the knowledge you acquired on earlier visits, or it might cause you to go back and re-acquire something you thought you had already learned. In either case, the list will have proved its worth as a learning aid.

#3 *Write every family member's name inside the book.*

If this is truly a "family dictionary," then *everyone* in the family must think of it as a personal possession. All of us tend to value things more, and care for things better, when we have a sense of ownership about them, and this applies to dictionaries, and other books, as well.

In writing each family member's name on the inside cover, or letting everyone print or sign his

Write family names in your dictionary

or her own name, you are also demonstrating that language learning is a family activity—equally important for adults as for children. This is a book that the family will share, and the lessons from it will be shared, too.

There is no clearer demonstration of a family's commitment to language improvement, and its desire to encourage language learning among all family members, than this signing of the family dictionary.

#4 *Never come back from a trip to the dictionary with just one word.*

You can go to the dictionary with just one word in mind, but why waste a glorious opportunity for learning on just a single word, when you can multiply your rewards many times over with only a little extra effort?

It is very difficult to learn anything about language one word a time. Improving your vocabulary—just like improving your spelling or pronunciation—is most efficiently and effectively accomplished when you can see patterns that apply throughout entire groups of words. If you can link your search for one word, in some way, with another that you associate or acquire during that same search, then you not only double your learning, but you greatly improve the chances that you will be able to recall whatever you learned when the need arises.

One of the simplest techniques for increasing the rewards that you derive from a trip to the dictionary is to get in the habit of looking a few words up, and a few words down, from the word you went to find. This gives you an opportunity to see what other interesting words might be in the neighborhood, and sometimes you will see connections between words that you never saw before. Such revelations occur rather frequently when the object of your search begins with a common prefix, such as *dis-, sub-, inter-,* and the like. For instance, you might have seen the word *prerequisite* used in a magazine article, and so you turned to that entry in your dictionary to help clarify its meaning or its pronunciation. Instead of ending your search there, however, you might also have noticed that this entry was situated among dozens of words that all begin with the letter combination *pre-,* which frequently derives from a Latin form that means "before" (just as a *pre*fix is something "fastened or affixed *before* or in front of the root word"). A *pre*requisite is "something that is required *before*hand; a prior condition."

- ***prerequisite***
- ***premature***
- ***premonition***
- ***presage***
- ***prerogative***

By scanning the entries above and below your object word, you will get a sense of how so many of these *pre-* words carry the meaning of "before" or "prior to" or "in front of" (for example, *premature, premonition,* and *presage*). But you may also bump into the word *prerogative,* and by lumping it into the other *pre-* words (its meaning of "an exclusive right or privilege" is derived from the Latin combination of "before" and "to ask"), you will always spell and pronounce this word with that initial *pre-*, instead of *per-*, as is often done by people who are not familiar with the word's origin or its position in the dictionary. So, you went looking for one word, and you came back with a basketful of others besides.

Another technique for helping you acquire several related words during a single trip to the dictionary is one that I call "Follow the Chain." It is simply a way of letting your dictionary itself stimulate your curiosity and suggest paths that you can take to widen and deepen your learning.

Have you ever consulted a dictionary for the definition of a word, only to find that word explained by other words that aren't in your vocabulary? Instead of letting this be the end of your particular investigation (and letting this discourage you from embarking on future investigations, as well), I suggest that you use it as a learning opportunity and as a way to increase the production from your original search.

- ***diatribe***
- ***invective***
- ***vehement***
- ***reproachful***

In one dictionary, for example, the word *diatribe* is defined as "a bitter and abusive criticism or denunciation; invective." If I allow myself to wonder whether I really know what an "invective" is, and if I realize that having the dictionary right in hand is an excellent opportunity to understand this word more clearly and to fix its meaning in my vocabulary, then I can focus on the entry for *invective* in just a matter of seconds. Within that definition I might come across the word *vehement*, or *reproachful*, and at these entries I would find other curious words that would lead me to other entries, and so on, and on, until the chain "breaks" or I decide to stop.

Of course, I could branch off in other directions at any point along the chain by employing some of the techniques I mentioned earlier. I could, for example, find myself at *invective* and decide to look a few words above and a few words below that particular entry. In doing so, I would come across *inveigh* and *inveigle;* applying the same technique at *reproachful* would yield *reprisal* and *reprobate*—all useful acquisitions.

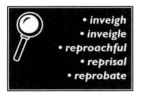

- *inveigh*
- *inveigle*
- *reproachful*
- *reprisal*
- *reprobate*

#5 *Always check the word origin that is included with each entry.*

Each dictionary uses special symbols and abbreviations to show where individual words came from and how they changed in form over time. You must become familiar with these symbols and abbreviations so that you can understand the wealth of information that your dictionary can provide, and you can do this by consulting the section in the very front of the book titled "Guide to the Dictionary" or "How to Use This Dictionary." The information you want will be found under the heading "Etymologies."

- etymology
- entomology

This word, *etymology* [pronounced ET-UH-MOLL-UH-JEE], which means "the origin or history of a word," is a useful one to add to your vocabulary, and to your children's vocabulary, as well, especially if you are going to be looking up word origins and word histories as a family. (Just be careful about pronouncing the first syllable so that you don't confuse the word with ***en**tomology,* which is the scientific study of insects.)

You may just be inquiring about a spelling—check the etymology, too. You may just be questioning a pronunciation or a definition—check the etymology, too. No matter what the object of your search happens to be, get in the habit of reading the origin and history that is given either at the beginning or the end of the entry.

Most of the etymologies you decipher won't prove very exciting and won't lead you to any greater understanding of spellings or meanings or usages. But every so often there will be one that will amaze you and will fill you with the excitement of learning; the world will seem somehow to make more sense, and you will want to share your new-found knowledge and understanding with others so that their world can make more sense to them. I find this feeling best expressed in the exclamation "AHA!"

I remember an "AHA!" that came over me when I read in my dictionary the etymology of the word *asterisk.* I went looking for this word because I had heard it pronounced "ass-ter-i**x**" so often that I wanted to see if perhaps there was an alternative spelling and pronunciation. There wasn't, and when I read the etymology, I knew why there wasn't, and I knew that I would never consider pronouncing or spelling the word with an *x* ever again.

• asterisk

Asterisk, you see, comes to us from the Greek word *aster*, meaning "star," and the suffix that the Greeks used to make things smaller, *-iskos*. To the Greeks, then, *asteriskos* meant "a little star," and that was precisely what I used to call that keyboard symbol before I learned it was an asterisk. The *-iskos* gives us that closing *s* and *k* in asterisk, and there is no *x* to be found anywhere. "AHA!"

• dilapidated

You'll find that many etymologies will be merely rewarding, instead of eye-popping, but that's reason enough to apply this rule to every search. For example, take the word *dilapidated*, which means "fallen into disrepair; decayed." Once you discover that at the heart of this word lies the Latin word *lapis*, meaning "stone," you will see why *dilapidated* customarily applies to buildings and to other constructions of stone or brick. Knowing this, you wouldn't choose to use *dilapidated* to describe an old overcoat, let's say, because your understanding of the etymology has given you a better, more refined, understanding of the word itself. You would choose a different adjective—perhaps *ragged, shopworn,* or *threadbare.*

Sometimes the etymology of your target word won't increase your knowledge or understanding much at all, but if you follow these last two suggestions together—that is, always check the etymology, even when you look a few words above and below your target word, and when you "follow the chain"—your odds of uncovering a rewarding or even a stunning nugget of knowledge improve considerably.

See if you get a special glow of understanding from the etymologies of the following words: *sophomore, malaria, assassin, companion.*

- ***sophomore***
- ***malaria***
- ***assassin***
- ***companion***

Dictionary Games and Activities

Most people think that "dictionary games" have to be formalized, standardized affairs that are governed by rules and that eventually separate winners from losers. But that is like saying that a father and child can't learn anything about baseball just by "playing catch" in the back yard, or that a child can't learn anything about basketball just by "shooting hoops" out in the driveway.

Play "The Dictionary Game"

Oh, there are "official" dictionary games, to be sure. The game of *Scrabble*™, in all its many forms, comes quickly to mind, and there are at least two other packaged board games—*Balderdash*™ and *Dictionary Dabble*™—that are based on a parlor game usually called "The Dictionary Game." This paper-and-pencil activity has been around for decades and can be played by groups large and small. It begins with one player selecting an obscure or totally unheard of word from the dictionary and copying its definition on a piece of paper. Each player now creates his or her own definition for that word and writes it down on a similar piece of paper. When the papers are collected, all the definitions are read aloud, and players vote for the definition they think is the actual one taken from the dictionary. Points are given for selecting the correct definition and for creating an incorrect definition that sounds so good that it makes other players think it is the correct definition.

"The Dictionary Game" can be a lot of fun, but it can also be rather daunting, and occasionally embarrassing, to those who are comparatively unfamiliar with the style and language commonly used in dictionary definitions. Think of this game as one that you and your children will grow into, and eventually enjoy as your knowledge of dictionaries and dictionary definitions grows. But to start that growth and to hone your dictionary skills, you need to have the functional equivalents to "playing catch" and "shooting hoops" at your family's disposal.

Hit the Target Word.

Here's a dictionary activity that's not really a "game" at all, yet it is fun, challenging, and it helps reinforce your knowledge of the alphabet quickly and without having to go through the "A-B-C-D..." song every time. All you do is to try opening your dictionary to a place that is as close as possible to the page that contains the entry word you are seeking. (If your dictionary has a thumb-index, just ignore it and select a page by looking at the dictionary from the top instead of the side.)

Estimate where an entry word will be found

Let's say you wanted to find the meaning of the word *myopia* [MY-OH-PEE-UH] because you had read the phrase "...our senator's *myopia* concerning budgetary deficits" in a newspaper column. If you know that there are 26 letters in the English alphabet, you could group the first 13 (*A* through *M*) in the first half, and the last 13 (*N* through *Z*) in the second. *Myopia,* then, would fall at the end of the m's, and so would be near the very middle of the alphabet.

Estimate the location of *myopia*

But if you open your dictionary to its exact middle, you'll likely find yourself somewhere in the *l*'s, perhaps a hundred pages in front of the one on which *myopia* appears. What happened?

What happened was that you just learned something about your alphabet and your language.

There are many more common English words that begin with the letters *A–M* than there are with *N–Z.* Thumb through your dictionary to see which letters take up the most pages, and which take up the fewest. Now take a stab at locating *myopia* again. How close did you come this time?

Here are a few more entry words to try using as targets and coming as close to as you can on your first try. Can your child make a more accurate stab then you did?

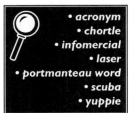

Estimate the location of *scuba, chortle, laser, infomercial,* and *yuppie*

scuba chortle laser
infomercial yuppie

When you locate these entry words, check their etymologies (Rule #5). Some were created by using the initial letters of other words—these are called *acronyms;* the others were created by combining or blending two words into one—these are called *portmanteau words* [pronounced PORT-MAN-TOE]. Which ones are acronyms; which are portmanteau words, and why are they called portmanteau words, anyway?

- ***acronym***
- ***chortle***
- ***infomercial***
- ***laser***
- ***portmanteau word***
- ***scuba***
- ***yuppie***

Reverse Dictionary Game.

I said that I thought the parlor activity called "The Dictionary Game" was too demanding for most children and for adults who are only beginning to develop their dictionary skills. But families can get great fun and benefit by just turning the game around. One person reads a dictionary definition while the other players try to guess the entry word to which that definition applies.

Guess the entry word from the definition

For example, could you guess what words are being described by the following definitions?

1. "a machine with a heavy blade that falls freely between upright guides to behead a condemned prisoner" (*Webster's II New College Dictionary*)
2. "a two-dimensional representation of the outline of an object, as a person's profile, filled in with black or another color" (*Random House Webster's College Dictionary*)
3. "the hair on a man's face, just in front of the ears, especially when the rest of the beard is cut off" (*Webster's New World Dictionary*)
4. "A colorless, poisonous narcotic alkaloid present in tobacco" (*The Concise Oxford Dictionary*)

(Answers: 1. *guillotine;* 2. *silhouette;* 3. *sideburns;* 4. *nicotine.* The etymologies for these words will show that all of them are derived from the names of real people, as are the words *sandwich, saxophone, lynch, boycott,* and many others, as well.)

- ***guillotine***
- ***silhouette***
- ***sideburns***
- ***nicotine***
- ***sandwich***
- ***saxophone***
- ***lynch***
- ***boycott***

Trade turns with your children in reading definitions and guessing entry words. If the correct answer isn't guessed on the first try, read another definition for the word, if there is one, or reveal the first letter in the entry word as a hint.

At Random.

Richard Armour, in his book titled *Educated Guesses* [370.1 ARM], describes a game that he used to stimulate interest among the students in a college writing course he was teaching.

The inspiration for this activity came to him one day when he, purely by chance, turned his dictionary to the page that contained the word *randem*—not *random*, but *randem*. He had never heard or seen this word before, but the dictionary told him that it is an adjective describing three horses that are harnessed to a vehicle, one behind the other. He knew that two horses, or people, or wheels, tied together in this way are said to be in *tandem*, so this new word, *randem*, filled a hole in his vocabulary by providing a perfectly sensible, one-word description of a situation that would take at least several words to explain without it.

Find an interesting word on a randomly selected page

• fortuitous
• fortunate

Invigorated by his fortuitous find, (use your dictionary to learn the distinction between *fortuitous* and *fortunate*), he made another random stab, this time opening to a page where he found *slubberdegullian*, which was defined as "a base and slovenly bore." Another new addition to his vocabulary, and this one he might find a use for right away.

He brought this activity into his classes and made it part of his students' daily routine. Each was required to randomly choose a dictionary page, to peruse that page for a novel or interesting word, and report to the class about that word and why it was chosen.

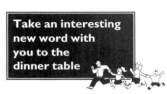

Take an interesting new word with you to the dinner table

Richard Armour suggests that this activity could also be used in high-school English classes, but I think it could work in a family setting, as well. Children and parents could come to the dinner table armed with one new or interesting word that they found by flipping through the pages of their "family dictionary." Maybe it was the history of the word that made it interesting, or perhaps it contains an unusual sequence of letters (see "Word Records" on page 109).

Branch out from the Root.

Sometimes, when you read an etymology, the root on which a particular word is based will make perfect sense, and you'll see very clearly how the meaning of the root is contained in the meaning of the word itself. For example, when you find that the word *spectator* is derived from the Latin word

- *spectacles*
- *spectrum*
- *inspect*
- *respect*
- *speculate*
- *specify*

- *unicorn*
- *uniform*
- *unify*
- *unique*
- *unison*

- *biceps*
- *bicuspid*
- *bifocal*
- *bifurcate*
- *bigamy*
- *binoculars*

- *triage*
- *trident*
- *trinity*
- *tripod*
- *trivet*
- *trivial*

spectare, meaning "to look at or see," you understand right away how the meaning of *spectator* ("one who watches or observes an event") and its Latin ancestor are related.

But now take one additional step and ask yourself if there might be a similar meaning ("to look at or see") at the heart of other familiar *spec-* or *spect-* words. How about the *spectacles* you wear to read the newspaper, or the *spectrum* of colors into which white light can be broken? Can you see any possible connections between "to look at or see" and the meanings of *inspect, respect, speculate,* and *specify*? Actually, there are 246 English words that derive from this one Latin root.

Or, let's focus in on roots that have numbers in them. The prefixes in *unicycle, bicycle,* and *tricycle* tell us the number of wheels (Latin *cyclus,* meaning "circles") on each vehicle. So, turn to the *uni-* pages in your dictionary and see whether there are other words that include the idea of "one" in their definitions. (Check out *unicorn, uniform, unify, unique, unison.*)

Now let's look at the *bi-* words that have something to do with "two" (*biceps, bicuspid, bifocal, bifurcate, bigamy, binoculars*). And the *tri-* words that contain in their meanings the idea of "three" (*triage, trident, trinity, tripod, trivet, trivial*).

With the help of books like Robert Schleifer's *Grow Your Vocabulary,* in the 428.1 section of your public library, you can create a list of the prefixes that carry the meanings 1 through 10. Now go back and forth with your child, each of you coming up with a different word for a particular number category. When someone is stumped, a trip to the dictionary will get that person right back into the game.

Take turns finding words having numbers in their prefix

Word Records.

A mathematician once told me that he could find something interesting, something special, about any number I might suggest. For example, the number 137 is composed entirely of digits that are prime numbers; 19,061 reads the same right side up or upside down; and so on.

Well, I think that every single word just might be special, too—that if we thought about a word long enough, we could find something notable, remarkable, or even unique in the pattern of its letters. But before you challenge me, or challenge yourself, to find the peculiar aspect of some thoroughly ordinary word, let's look at some of the ways that words can achieve "special" status and can make themselves noteworthy in our minds and memories.

Take the word *revolutionary,* for example. Here is a word that contains all the five vowels (*a, e, i, o, u*) and the letter *y.* Do you think it is possible that there is another word that might also belong to this special group? "Yes, *unquestionably,*" you reply (and so there is). But perhaps you and your child might start out by excluding the letter *y* and just keeping an ongoing list of words—tucked inside your "family dictionary"—whose spellings include all five vowels. When you come across, or think about, a new one, you add it to the list (and look it up in your dictionary, too).

Keep a list of words that include all five vowels

What is the longest word you can find that has only one vowel? Make another list for this category and keep adding to it (there's one such word that is nine letters long). What is the longest word you can find that is pronounced with only one syllable? Another list. Well, you get the idea.

Keep lists of other special or interesting words

Dave Morice lists dozens of such categories, which he calls "Word Records," in his 1997 book titled *Alphabet Avenue* [793.734 MOR], and Gyles Brandreth lists others in *The Joy of Lex* [793.73 BRA].

There are hundreds of other games and activities that you can enjoy with your family that will also stimulate wordplay and encourage dictionary use in your home. I included many of them in the "Language" unit of *Family Learning: How to Help Your Children Succeed in School by Learning at Home* [371.042 RUS], and you'll find many others in the books I have listed in "Useful Family Resources" on pages 113–114.

But the purpose of all these activities is the same: to create an atmosphere in the home in which learning—especially learning about language—is seen as an unexceptional part of everyday living. As I pointed out in *Family Learning,*

> "Parents can open a world of opportunity for their children just by showing a consistent respect and admiration for the skillful and artful use of Standard English. By listening and reading, by examining everything they hear or read, they can demonstrate that learning about language is a lifelong pursuit and that skill in speaking and writing is worth pursuing."

USEFUL FAMILY RESOURCES

The Dewey classification numbers that are shown in brackets at the end of each listing may not correspond to the ones used by your public library. Even so, they will lead you to areas within your library that may include other useful resources for you and your family.

Alphabet Avenue: Wordplay in the Fast Lane, by Dave Morice (Chicago: Chicago Review Press, 1997) [793.73 MOR].

The Appropriate Word: Finding the Best Way to Say What You Mean, by J. N. Hook (Reading, Mass.: Addison-Wesley Publishing Co., 1990) [428 HOO].

The Big Book of Beastly Mispronunciations, by Charles Harrington Elster (Boston: Houghton Mifflin Co., 1999) [423.1 ELS].

Dos, Donts & Maybes of English Usage, by Theodore M. Bernstein (New York: Times Books, 1977) [428 BER].

Educated Guesses: Light / Serious Suggestions for Parents and Teachers, by Richard Armour (Santa Barbara, Cal.: Woodbridge Press, 1983) [370.1 ARM].

The Elements of Style, Third Edition, by William Strunk, Jr. and E. B. White (New York: Macmillan Publishing Co., 1979) [808 STR].

Family Learning: How to Help Your Children Succeed in School by Learning at Home, by William F. Russell, Ed.D. (St. Charles, Ill.: First Word Learning Systems, Inc., 1997) [371.042 RUS].

Grow Your Vocabulary: By Learning the Roots of English Words, by Robert Schleifer (New York: Random House, 1995) [428.1 SCH].

Heavens to Betsy! and Other Curious Sayings, by Charles Earle Funk (New York: Harper & Row, Publishers, 1955) [422 FUN].

In Other Words: Making Better Word Choices in American English, by Anne Bertram (Lincolnwood, Ill.: NTC Publishing Group, 1997) [423.1 BER].

Is There a Cow in Moscow? by Charles Harrington Elster (New York: Collier Books, 1990) [421.54 ELS].

Sleeping Dogs Don't Lay: Practical Advice for the Grammatically Challenged, by Richard Lederer and Richard Dowis (New York: St. Martin's Press, 1999) [428.2 LED].

The Joy of Lex: How to Have Fun with 860,341,500 Words, by Gyles Brandreth (New York: William Morrow & Co., 1980) [793.73 BRA].

The Story Behind the Word, by Morton S. Freeman (Philadelphia: ISI Press, 1985) [422.03 FRE].

Thereby Hangs a Tale: Stories of Curious Word Origins, by Charles Earle Funk (New York: Harper & Row, Publishers, 1950) [422 FUN].

There Is No Zoo in Zoology, by Charles Harrington Elster (New York: Collier Books, 1988) [421.54 ELS].

Van Winkle's Return: Change in American English, 1966–1986, by Kenneth G. Wilson (Hanover, N.H.: University Press of New England, 1987) [428 WIL].

When Is a Pig a Hog? by Bernice Randall (New York: Prentice Hall, 1991) [422.03 RAN].

Woe Is I, by Patricia T. O'Conner (New York: G. P. Putnam's Sons, 1996) [428.2 OCO].

Word Mysteries & Histories, by the Editors of The American Heritage Dictionaries (Boston: Houghton Mifflin Co., 1986) [422.03 WOR].

Word Origins and Their Romantic Stories, by Wilfred Funk (New York: Bell Publishing Co., 1950) [422 FUN].

The Words You Should Know, by David Olsen (Holbrook, Mass.: Adams Media Corp., 1991) [428.1 OLS].

INDEX

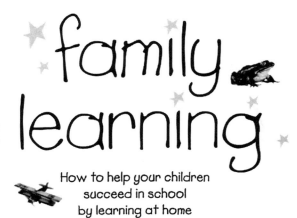